C000128103

WJEC/Eduqas

Religious Studies
for A Level Year 1 & AS

Philosophy of Religion

Revision Guide

Gregory A. Barker and Richard Gray

Illuminate
Publishing

WJEC/Eduqas

Religious Studies
for A Level Year 1 & AS

Philosophy
of Religion

Revision Guide

Gregory A. Barker and Richard Gray

Published in 2019 by Illuminate Publishing Ltd, P.O. Box 1160, Cheltenham, Gloucestershire GL50 9RW

Orders: Please visit www.illuminatepublishing.com

or email sales@illuminatepublishing.com

British Library Cataloguing in Publication Data

A catalogue record for this book is available from the British Library

ISBN 978-1-911208-67-9

Printed by Standartų Spaustuvė, Lithuania

01.19

The publisher's policy is to use papers that are natural, renewable and recyclable products made from wood grown in sustainable forests. The logging and manufacturing processes are expected to conform to the environmental regulations of the country of origin.

Every effort has been made to contact copyright holders of material reproduced in this book. If notified, the publishers will be pleased to rectify any errors or omissions at the earliest opportunity.

Editor: Geoff Tuttle

Design and Layout: John Dickinson Graphic Design

Cover design: EMC Design Ltd, Bedford

Cover image: Skarie20 / iStock

Photo acknowledgements

p.1 Skarie20 / iStock; p.6 NikoNomad; p.7 Historic Collection / Alamy Stock Photo; p.9 Zoran Karapancev; p.12 Ivan Smuk; p.13 Nuamfolio; p.15 (left) Albert H. Teich; p.15 (right) Creative Commons; p.18 chrisdorney; p.19 Nicku; p.21 Creative Commons; p.24 (top) TLaoPhotography; p.24 (bottom left to right) kyselova Inna, fortton, Sarah 2, p.25 (left to right) foodonwhite, FocusStocker, Sangaroon, Jan Martin Will, Valery 121283, Akugasahagy, Katy Luck; p.27 Ezume Images; p.30 (top) RecycleMan; p.30 (bottom) thaisign; p.31 Orla; p.33 Elnur; p.36 Creative Commons; p.37 Hafiez Razalie; p.39 Vasily Deyneka; p.44 The Prosblogian; p.45 Courtesy Gregory Paul; p.47 Song_about_summer; p.50 Andrey_Popov; p.53 FOTOKITA; p.55 Banauke; p.58 John Hick - Is Death Final? / Closer to Truth / YouTube; p.59 Everett Historical / Shutterstock.com; p.61 Inked Pixels; p.65 HQuality; p.67 Frank Gaertner; p.70 vchal; p.71 Radachynskyi Serhii; p.73 Chris_Wang; p.76 nelen; p.77 pp1; p.79 Lightspring

Contents

About Trigger revision

How do I manage all of the information?

We've created these revision guides to help you manage all of the content that you have learned in your A-Level studies and help apply this to an exam.

Thus, these guides are different from a textbook. Textbooks develop your skills of knowledge and understanding and are supported by evidence and examples. They also equip you with the skills of critical analysis and evaluation in response to the issues relevant to the content so that you can form your own judgements. The Illuminate textbooks also contain ways that you can work with the content to organise and present material in an effective way.

A revision guide, however, prepares you for the final hurdle: transporting everything you have learned into an exam situation.

One of the challenges of this A-Level course has been managing the sheer amount of information from the themes you have studied. One traditional way of doing this is to reduce the material into a condensed block of notes. This can be very useful as a way to summarise the content but may still leave you without a way to manage, remember and also effectively transfer material in an examination situation. This is why we recommend the Trigger concept.

The Trigger concept

A 'Trigger' is simply a way of prompting the 'unpacking' or 'downloading' of the information required for an examination, that is, the basic materials to display your AO1 and AO2 skills.

A Trigger is not the same as a key term. A Trigger tends to indicate something essential but also points beyond itself for further development. However, some key terms are quite naturally Triggers whilst others are contained within the Triggers.

How does a set of Triggers work?

Our Trigger concept helps with memory stimulation and further development. It is like a reverse cloze exercise – instead of filling in words in a text, the Triggers are presented, and the rest of the text has to be added! The task, then, is to create activities that can help fill the gaps around the missing text by utilising the Triggers you have.

Create your own zip Trigger lists on your mobile devices to help you revise before entering the examination.

Benefits of Triggers

Triggers are:

- Portable (easily transferable to an examination)
- Convenient, practical and readily accessible (something simple enough to transfer to a portable device)
- Concise and efficient (compact and manageable)
- Precise (accurate, focused on the vital elements).

How to use this book

1. Choose a subtheme and read through the Knowledge and Understanding area; you will notice that the Triggers are highlighted.
2. Now, go to the AO1 Activity for that subtheme. This asks you to work with a 'zip file' image of the Triggers. You will create your own lists and definitions; sometimes you will be asked to find missing Triggers or to create the 'zip file' for yourself.
3. Read though the Evaluation section. Take note of the Triggers (these are always presented in terms of controversies).
4. You are now ready to take on the AO2 activities for that subtheme, studying the 'zip files' we have presented and creating your own lists, definitions and notes. Sometimes, we will ask you to find missing Triggers or to create the 'zip file' for yourself.
5. At the end of this book you will see examples of Triggers at work in AO1 and AO2 responses. There are also practical insights to help you with your examination.

Key features

In each theme

Specification Link – relevant to the subtheme
AO1 Knowledge – the most essential aspects of AO1 elements from the specification
AO2 Evaluation – the most essential AO2 material, highlighting three specific controversies for each Specification issue
Triggers – words for AO1 and AO2 highlighted in the main text and then presented in a zip file graphic
Trigger Quotes – easily memorisable short quotations that can be applied to an exam response
Quick Revision – ideas to help you get ready for the exam
Spotlight: Evaluative judgements – insights you can use to form a judgement
Trigger activities – these help you to unpack and use the Triggers as a basis for an answer

At the end of the book

Using Triggers to create exam answers – examples of Triggers helping to create a suitable answer
Synoptic Links – examples of how other areas of the Specification can enhance or support answers
AO1 responses: essential guidance
AO2 responses: essential guidance

These sections share insights to help you respond to the WJEC/Eduqas Specification requirements.

We are excited by these books and hope they will help ease the burden and enable you to manage effectively the content involved in the new A Level.

Richard Gray
Dr Greg Barker

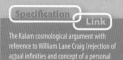

Specification Link

The Kalam cosmological argument with reference to William Lane Craig (rejection of actual infinities and concept of a personal creator).

AO1
What is ...
Knowledge and understanding

AO2
What is ...
Evaluation and critical analysis

...rd way: contingency and necessity
...e world consists of **contingent beings** they are t...
...ve the possibility of not existing.
...erefore, at one time there must have been no bei...

TRIGGER QUOTE

The only way to have an eternal cause but a temporal effect would seem to be if the cause is a personal agent who freely chooses to create an effect in time. **(W. L. Craig)**

Quick Revision

Try to respond to each of the controversies with your own thought and commentary. Think about the evidence you...

Spotlight:

AO1 Trigger revis...

A

Inductive arguments and the...

| inductive | contingent | everythin... |
| a posteriori | 'argument' and | universe... |

Arguments for the existence of God – inductive

Specification Link

Inductive arguments – cosmological: inductive proofs; the concept of 'a posteriori'. Aquinas first three ways – (motion or change; cause and effect; contingency and necessity).

AO1

What is …
Knowledge and understanding

This is the skill that involves *selecting* the relevant and appropriate information, *organising* it and then *presenting* it through a *personal explanation* that may involve the use of supporting *evidence* and *examples*.

Spot the Triggers!
The words in blue are Triggers – key words and phrases that can help you remember knowledge and understanding in this area.

TIP

The cosmological arguments for God's existence focus on a single point of origin in order to explain the universe.

Theme 1A: Inductive arguments – cosmological

The nature of induction

- The cosmological argument is an **inductive** argument.
- Inductive reasoning is **a posteriori** (post experience) because it depends upon **empirical** (derived from the senses) evidence and experience that leads to a possible conclusion.
- Therefore, the cosmological argument bases its inductive argument on empirical evidence – what is before us – to arrive at a probable conclusion as to the origin of the **universe**.
- The cosmological argument uses the evidence of the existing universe and asks the question 'Where did it come from?' or 'Is there a **First Cause**?' as the basis for its argument.
- The cosmological argument observes that our world is a **contingent** world, full of change and that exists within the dimensions of space and time. This is where the argument begins its analysis.
- It is important to distinguish between an **'argument' and 'reasoning'**. An argument can be inductive overall but use reasoning that is concerned with deductive statements as a part of its strategy. For example, the Kalam is often claimed to be a deductive argument. This is not true. It does contain elements of deductive reasoning (e.g. actual and potential infinites) but this does not make it a deductive argument overall.

Aquinas' first three ways

First way: motion (or change)

- An object has the **potential** to become something different, to change.
- **Motion** fulfils that potential into an actual entity.
- Nothing can be both potential and **actual** at the same time.
- Whatever is moved must be moved by something different that is actual (an **efficient cause**).
- The chain of movers cannot be traced back infinitely (**infinite regress**), since then there would be no actual first mover.
- As there is movement now there must be a **First Mover**, moved by no other.
- According to Aquinas, this First Mover is what we understand to be God.

Second way: cause

- ◼ Nothing that exists could be the efficient cause of itself, i.e. both actual and potential. That is, an existing thing is caused by **another cause** and not itself. It is **not self-caused**.
- ◼ It would already have had to exist to bring itself into existence; this is **illogical**.
- ◼ Infinite regress of causes means there would be no **First Cause** (and so no other causes).
- ◼ Therefore, if we trace causes back far enough, there must be a First Cause, caused by no other. In other words, the origin of all things must be **self-caused**.
- ◼ According to Aquinas, this is what we understand to be **God**.

Third way: contingency and necessity

- ◼ The world consists of **contingent beings**; they are **temporary** and have the possibility of not existing.
- ◼ Therefore, at one time there must have been no being / **nothing in existence**. Therefore, there would be nothing that could bring anything into existence.
- ◼ Hence an infinite regress of temporary/contingent movement, cause and being is impossible because this **cannot explain now** why these things exist.
- ◼ As there are contingent beings existing now, there must be something non-contingent (or a **necessary** 'thing' must exist).
- ◼ According to Aquinas, this is what we understand to be God.

The Kalam cosmological argument with reference to William Lane Craig

- ◼ In 1993 William Lane Craig put forward an argument that developed the basic principles of the cosmological argument.
- ◼ Craig developed this from an **ancient Arabic argument** called the **Kalam** argument.
- ◼ **Everything has a cause** of its existence (temporal and temporary).
- ◼ The **universe began** to exist and therefore, the universe has a cause of its existence.
- ◼ Since **no scientific explanation** can provide a **causal account** of the origin of the universe, the cause must be personal (explanation is given in terms of a personal agent).
- ◼ The only challenge to the first cause was an **infinite regress**.
- ◼ Craig argued that an **actual infinite** of temporal events or causes cannot exist.
- ◼ He compared it to a **library** with an actually infinite number of books.
- ◼ If books were of two infinite types (**red and black**) the combined total would be same as the sum of each type which is an absurdity.
- ◼ Craig argued also that there was a different type of infinity, a **potential infinite**, to which temporal events can still be added.
- ◼ The actual infinite is impossible, according to Craig, but a potential infinite is possible.
- ◼ Craig argued that if an actual infinite was impossible, a potential infinite **confirms a First Cause** – the fact that the universe had a beginning.

❝TRIGGER QUOTES❞

Motion is nothing else than the reduction of something from potentiality to actuality.
(T. Aquinas)

There is no case known ... in which a thing is found to be the efficient cause of itself; for so it would be prior to itself, which is impossible. **(T. Aquinas)**

Quick Revision

Select what you think are the five most important Triggers as presented by Aquinas and Craig and explain why they are important to our understanding of the cosmological argument.

Specification Link

The Kalam cosmological argument with reference to William Lane Craig (rejection of actual infinities and concept of a personal creator).

❝TRIGGER QUOTE❞

I think that it can be plausibly argued that the cause of the universe must be a personal Creator. For how else could a temporal effect arise from an eternal cause? **(W. L. Craig)**

Al-Ghazali is often attributed with compiling the Kalam argument for the existence of God.

AO2

What is ...
Evaluation and critical analysis ?

The AO2 skills of evaluation and critical analysis mean engaging with the controversies surrounding a subject. This is more than merely describing or listing the points made about a controversy. To achieve this, one weighs up strengths and weaknesses of various sides and takes a position. On the right are three controversies for each issue – you can engage in these by extending their arguments (adding examples, quotes or other details), weighing up their strengths and weaknesses, and coming to a conclusion.

'TRIGGER QUOTES'

Empiricists claim that sense experience is the ultimate source of all our concepts and knowledge. **(J. Mackie)**

The essence of life is a statistical probability on a colossal scale. **(R. Dawkins)**

Using quotes
A quote can strengthen an argument you are making – but always be sure to include a sentence as to why the quote is important/relevant.

TIP

Issue:
Whether inductive arguments for God's existence are persuasive

Three evaluative controversies!

- **Controversy 1: *Are evidence-based arguments more persuasive than arguments not based on evidence?***
  Inductive arguments are empirical with arguably a scientific methodology and therefore this makes them credible, especially in the 21st century and the **modern world**. They deal with real things that are before us that we experience and can relate to. One could argue they are superior to arguments not based on evidence because they are not theoretical. However, it could be argued that the inductive methodology can contain **faulty reasoning** when there are such a variety of possible explanations, which creates doubt and **not certainty** of any kind.

- **Controversy 2: *Does the cumulative force of evidence-based arguments make the cosmological arguments persuasive?***
  There are **different explanations** for cosmological arguments and although slightly different, it does mean that they support each other with the **same conclusion** of a First Cause. There may be different understandings as to the exact nature of this First Cause but it does allow for a possibility (or arguably the probability) that this could be a **creator God**. This flexible reasoning means it can be approached from different directions, for example Aquinas' three ways, but the conclusion is not undermined by this. However, one could argue that such alternative and various ways of reasoning to support the same conclusion actually weaken the conclusion.

- **Controversy 3: *Is a First Cause a credible conclusion?***
  The main advantage with inductive arguments for the existence of God is that they create a **possibility** for the conclusion being that God is the First Cause. However, for some this is also a disadvantage because the nature of inductive arguments and the cosmological argument in particular is that we can happily accept all the evidence and reasoning but simultaneously **reject the conclusion** without contradiction. In this case the conclusion to the argument becomes more of a **groundless explanation** at worst or at the very least uncertain, which then significantly weakens the whole point of the argument.

Sp●tlight: **Evaluative judgements**
This section contains a special insight that you can use to form a judgement.

Some, like Richard Dawkins, would argue that although science involves inductive reasoning, its success is crucially dependent upon the force of probability of the conclusions themselves. To argue that it is possible for there to be a tiger outside my front door does not carry the same force as the possibility of there not being one there! Therefore, any inductive arguments are measured by how credible the reasoning and conclusions are at each stage of the argument.

Issue:

The extent to which the Kalam cosmological argument is convincing

▣ **Controversy 1: *Is Craig's version of the Kalam appealing because it has the* benefits of modern science *for support?***

It could be argued that the main strength of Craig's Kalam is that he does draw upon modern scientific understanding to aid his argument. Most scientific theories as to the origins of the universe propose a **Big Bang** theory and accept that the universe had a point of origin often called a **cosmic singularity**. This would suggest that the universe is **finite**, or at least potentially infinite as in Craig's understanding. However, not all agree in Craig's analysis of cause, especially with the advancement in understanding of the nature of quantum physics that challenges our whole understanding of causal principles when at a subatomic level they seem to be absent!

▣ **Controversy 2: *Is the Kalam argument* theologically biased?***

Craig's argument can be very convincing for the theist, so much so that one could argue that it is **not objective** and simply a **manipulation** of reason to support an intended end. Philosophers, such as Mackie, have challenged the very first premise of the argument that we assume everything that exists has a cause for its existence and although this has been hotly debated in philosophy, it does demonstrate that there are aspects of Craig's argument that are **not universally accepted**. Therefore, the extent to which the Kalam cosmological argument may be convincing could be argued to be directly influenced by one's personal religious beliefs.

▣ **Controversy 3: *Is the conclusion of a* personal creator *the only acceptable line of reasoning?***

Craig's argument that since the **physical laws** of the universe – which did not exist prior to the universe itself – cannot explain the creation or cause of the universe, then the only viable explanation is some **independent**, self-existing and self-contained entity which can then only be explained by the idea of a **personal God**. This last line of reasoning – that the self-existing and self-contained entity can only be adequately explained by a personal creator God – does appeal to many theists but is a personal God the only alternative? Some challenge this as a false dichotomy.

> **❝TRIGGER QUOTE❞**
>
> The only way to have an eternal cause but a temporal effect would seem to be if the cause is a personal agent who freely chooses to create an effect in time. **(W. L. Craig)**

String theory suggests there may well be multiple parallel universes!

Sp●tlight: Evaluative judgements

This section contains a special insight that you can use to form a judgement.

Recent developments in our understanding of the universe by popular physicists, such as Brian Greene, propose that string theory presents us with the idea of different dimensions to the universe. This even allows for the possibility of multiple universes. Would each one have a First Cause? If so, would this First Cause be the same First Cause?

Quick Revision

Try to respond to each of the controversies with your own thought and commentary. Think about the evidence you would provide to support your reasoning.

AO1 Trigger revision activity

A

ZIP

Inductive arguments and the Kalam argument

inductive	contingent	everything has a cause	actual infinite
a posteriori	'argument' and 'reasoning'	universe began	library
empirical	ancient Arabic argument	no scientific explanation	red and black
universe		causal account	potential infinite
First Cause	Kalam	infinite regress	confirms a First Cause

1 Here is your zip file of portable Triggers. →

2 Practise 'downloading' your zip file of Triggers from memory. See how many you can recall on first attempt. →

3 When you are confident enough, order the Triggers into a list as you may do in an examination situation.

Why Trigger?
Remember, your Triggers are to help you transfer your knowledge and understanding in a manageable, efficient and portable manner.

TIP

5 Now read through your descriptions and think about ways in which you could develop these using your Trigger quotes. ←

4 Attempt to write one clear sentence to define each Trigger.

B

ZIP

Aquinas three ways

God	another cause	First Cause	cannot explain now
temporary	illogical	potential	necessary
efficient cause	not self-caused	nothing in existence	motion
			actual

1 Fix the zip file! There are four Triggers missing from this zip file – find them and add them in. →

2 There's another problem: the Triggers are out of order! Put them in the same order as they appear in the AO1 section above. →

3 Practise 'downloading' your zip file of Triggers from memory. See how many you can recall on first attempt.

6 Now read through your definitions and think about ways in which you could develop these using your Trigger quotes. ←

5 Attempt to write one clear sentence to define each Trigger. ←

4 When you are confident enough, order the Triggers into a list as you may do in an examination situation.

AO2 Trigger revision activity

A ZIP

The persuasive nature of inductive arguments

evidence-based	cumulative force	credible conclusion
modern world	different explanations	possibility
faulty reasoning	same conclusion	reject the conclusion
not certainty	creator God	groundless explanation

1 Here is your zip file of portable Triggers.

2 Practise 'downloading' your zip file of Triggers from memory. See how many you can recall on first attempt.

3 When you are confident enough, order the Triggers into a list as you may do in an examination situation.

5 Now read through all your sentences and think about ways in which you could develop these using your Trigger quotes, further examples, and noting strengths and weaknesses.

4 'Double-click' each Trigger in your memory – what can you say about an evaluative point of view in a clear sentence? Write this down. Do this for each Trigger in turn.

REVISION TIP

Using Trigger quotes
When you choose the Trigger quotes that you wish to use make sure that you explain how they are relevant.

B ZIP

Is the Kalam argument convincing?

benefits of modern science	theologically biased?	personal God
finite	not objective	independent
cosmic singularity	personal creator	

1 Fix the zip file! There are four Triggers missing from this zip file – find them and add them in.

2 There's another problem: the Triggers are out of order! Put them in the same order as they appear in the AO2 section above.

3 Practise 'downloading' your zip file of Triggers from memory. See how many you can recall on first attempt.

6 Now read through all your sentences and think about ways in which you could develop these using your Trigger quotes, further examples, and noting strengths and weaknesses.

5 Attempt to write one clear sentence to define each Trigger.

4 When you are confident enough, order the Triggers into a list as you may do in an examination situation.

11

Specification **Link**

Inductive arguments – teleological: St Thomas Aquinas' Fifth Way – concept of governance; archer and arrow analogy.

AO1

What is ... Knowledge and understanding **?**

This is the skill that involves *selecting* the relevant and appropriate information, *organising* it and then *presenting* it through a *personal explanation* that may involve the use of supporting *evidence* and *examples*.

TIP

Answers often begin their account of Aquinas' argument (or those by Paley and Tennant) with a lengthy paragraph recounting irrelevant biographical details. Credit is given for the demonstration of an understanding of the arguments, not for potted biographies.

The archer is the intelligent cause behind the arrow.

Theme 1B: Inductive arguments – teleological

The teleological argument

The design argument is also referred to as the teleological argument. It implies the existence of God from particular characteristics evident in observing the world. The arguments from Aquinas and Paley focus on the following characteristics:

- **Order and regularity**: the nature of the universe seems ordered and it seems to work to definable rules (laws of nature). It is therefore predictable because this order is achieved by acting in a regular and consistent way.
- **Purpose**: the order and regularity do not seem aimless but, rather, there seems to be some (end) goal or purpose.

St Thomas Aquinas' Fifth Way (teleological argument)

Aquinas viewed nature as a coordinated complex of entities working toward the realisation of ends that are internal to their own natures. .

His argument can be summarised thus:

- There are things without knowledge that act for ends.
- If something without knowledge acts for an end, then it must be because it is **directed** by a being with knowledge and intelligence.
- Just as an **archer** (intelligent being) aims and directs the **arrow** (an object without knowledge), the **universe** also works by **natural laws** (which in themselves possess no intelligence) and therefore require some initial intelligence for direction.
- Therefore, there must be an intelligent being by whom natural things within the universe are directed towards their ends.
- This **ultimate intelligent being** we call God.

TRIGGER QUOTES

Whatever lacks knowledge cannot move towards an end, unless it is directed by some being endowed with knowledge and intelligence. **(T. Aquinas)**

So either the orderliness of nature is where all explanation stops, or we must postulate an agent of such great power and knowledge ... the simplest such agent ... God. **(R. Swinburne)**

William Paley's teleological argument

- Paley argued that if you chance upon a watch upon a heath, even if you had never seen a watch before, you would know that this instrument did not happen by **chance**; it must be something 'made', that is, the result of the work of an **intelligent mind**.
- All the parts fit together intricately and achieve the purpose of telling time.
- Therefore, there must have been a designer because there is **no alternative** naturalistic explanation.
- Likewise, the way the universe fits together for a purpose, demands an intelligent designer.
- For the universe the only explainable designer would have to be God.

Paley pointed out that the analogy still would work even if:
- We had **never seen** a watch before.
- We found that the mechanism did not always work perfectly or was **broken**.
- There were parts of the machine whose function we did **not understand**.

Paley also referred to the complex design of the **human eye**, being designed for the particular purpose of seeing, as evidence on its own for a designing intelligence.

Paley also argued that the way the **planets** obeyed laws in their movements and the general order and regularity observed in the universe according to fundamental laws and a **predictable** manner demanded an intelligent mind as explanation.

Specification Link

William Paley's watchmaker – analogy of complex design.

❝ TRIGGER QUOTE ❞

Were there no examples in the world of contrivance except the eye, it alone would be sufficient to support the conclusion ... of an intelligent creator. **(W. Paley)**

Quick Revision

Make a quick table with three columns and try to list the main concepts involved in each of the arguments given by the three scholars you find in this section.

Specification Link

F. R. Tennant's anthropic and aesthetic arguments – the universe specifically designed for intelligent human life.

Tennant's design argument

Tennant focused on different characteristics evident when observing the world:
- **Anthropic** principle: the goal or purpose of the world is **beneficial** for the flourishing of life.
- **Aesthetic** principle: the universe exhibits beauty; however, beauty is not a necessary feature for our survival. In itself it serves **no function** other than to satisfy human beings.

The anthropic principle

- The anthropic principle suggests that **nature provides** in advance for the needs of animals and humans.
- The main benefit from this order and regularity is to **sustain life**.
- The **precise conditions** for this are unbelievably complex and improbable and so appear to be geared specifically towards anthropic existence.
- There must be more than physical laws to account for the improbability of life. It suggests an **ultimate intelligence**.

The aesthetic argument

- Tennant argued that the universe is **infused with beauty** from the microscopic to the macroscopic. However, beauty is unnecessary because it has **no survival value** and yet still exists.
- No other species reacts to its surroundings in this way, for example, humans appreciate music, art and literature.
- For Tennant, the existence of beauty in the world was clear evidence that God exists and even encourages the **enquiring** mind to discover God.

Scientists argue that the probability of human life actually existing in the first place is incredibly low.

❝ TRIGGER QUOTES ❞

As we look out into the Universe ... it almost seems as if the Universe must in some sense have known that we were coming. **(F. Dyson)**

The aesthetic argument for theism becomes more persuasive when it renounces all claims to proof and appeals to a logical probability. **(F. R. Tennant)**

AO2

What is ...
Evaluation and critical analysis ?

The AO2 skills of evaluation and critical analysis mean engaging with the controversies surrounding a subject. This is more than merely describing or listing the points made about a controversy. To achieve this, one weighs up strengths and weaknesses of various sides and takes a position. On the right are three controversies for each issue – you can engage in these by extending their arguments (adding examples, quotes or other details), weighing up their strengths and weaknesses, and coming to a conclusion.

❝ TRIGGER QUOTES ❞

Anarchy and the reign of terror are overmatched in injustice, ruin, and death by a hurricane and a pestilence. **(J. S. Mill)**

... Darwin made it possible to be an intellectually fulfilled atheist. **(R. Dawkins)**

Using quotes
A quote can strengthen an argument you are making – but always be sure to include a sentence as to why the quote is important/relevant.

TIP

Issue:
The effectiveness of the teleological argument for God's existence

Three evaluative controversies!

■ **Controversy 1:** *Can a probable inductive argument ever be effective?*
Some argue that there is **strong support** from the observation that the sheer complexity of our universe, with its many life forms and complex, inter-connected systems that support life, indicates deliberate design from some almighty mind. However, this is only **one possible conclusion** and indeed, probable only for those who see it as a sensible and credible conclusion to draw from the evidence. In reality, there are many **other possible conclusions** that can be drawn from the evidence and this is a major weakness of the teleological argument.

■ **Controversy 2:** *Are the underlying assumptions of the teleological argument valid?*
The effectiveness of the analogies has long been questioned: is it appropriate to apply the analogies of an archer and a watch to the universe? Such analogies are often seen as **suspect** at best and the argument depends strongly on the assumption that such analogies are indeed accurate. If we **reject the assumption**, then we can reject the argument itself. Despite this, the contribution of Tennant, in introducing more scientific-based evidence seem to have given the teleological argument evidence more **credibility**.

■ **Controversy 3:** *What about the chaos and imperfections in the universe?*
In *Nature and Religion* (1874), Mill, following Hume's original observation, focused on the occurrence of disorder in the universe such as the various **atrocities in nature**. For Mill, the work of nature that is destructive and random shows that we do not live in a benevolent world designed by a moral God. The designer holds **personal responsibility** for the success or failure of that which is designed. In human terms we would demand justice. Can the designer therefore be benevolent? Obviously, this is where the role of **theodicies** come in for religious believers but it does raise the issue that the teleological argument does rely upon further assumptions to support it.

Sp●tlight: Evaluative judgements
This section contains a special insight that you can use to form a judgement.

Thinkers such as Richard Dawkins reject the teleological argument, arguing that scientific evidence is stacked against it. However, some scientists do recognise the anthropic principle in terms of its evidence – that life as we know it was actually very improbable and yet it still occurred!

Issue:

Whether teleological arguments for God's existence are persuasive in the 21st century

◾ **Controversy 1: *There are alternative explanations***
The 21st century is a modern scientific age and we have access to **advanced information**, ranging from evidence supporting the Big Bang theory, or an oscillating universe, the ideas of multiverses and also the insight gleaned from quantum mechanics. In addition to this, the theory of evolution gives a non-supernatural explanation and many have argued that this has filled the gap that necessitates a **God of the Gaps** explanation. However, do alternative explanations always require the rejection of a belief in God or can they add to the force of support for the belief in God? For instance, it could be argued that recent science recognises a finely balanced universe being maintained by '**cosmological constants**' such as the gravitational constant, the speed of light, the basic properties of elementary particles, and Planck's constant.

◾ **Controversy 2: *What counts as persuasive today?***
It can be argued that the teleological arguments tend to be expressed as **inductive** arguments and so are about **probabilities** and not about presenting (deductive) 'proof'. The strengths of the teleological arguments are that they actually provide a reasonable explanation for many people. Although the idea of a God of the Gaps may not be attractive to some, for others the persuasive nature of the teleological arguments is that they provide an explanation. For others, the universe remains **inexplicable** and we should just be able to accept that.

◾ **Controversy 3: *Part of the cumulative argument for God*.**
Professor **Richard Swinburne** argued that when all arguments for the existence of God are considered together, they all gather a **statistically cumulative force** and point to the same conclusion that there is a God. Swinburne also advocates that the simplest explanation is probably the best explanation. However, many would still question the **dubious correlations** between the nature of the evidence presented, which varies in terms of quality and quantity and rests upon selective rejections of alternative explanations.

Both Dawkins (against) and Swinburne (in support) provide strong views about the value of the teleological arguments.

Sp⬤tlight: Evaluative judgements

This section contains a special insight that you can use to form a judgement.

The teleological argument can be seen as persuasive if one accepts all its various strands together. In the same way, its persuasion is extended in light of Swinburne's cumulative argument. However, one has to question whether this is a truly philosophical or scientific approach. Maybe this approach is more like trying to explain what could have happened based upon minimal substantial evidence?

Quick Revision

Have a look at the six controversies you have just read. Try to think of two other controversies (lines of reasoning), one for each of the Specification areas, and consider the evidence that could be presented in the particular debates that you think of.

AO1 Trigger revision activity

A

ZIP

Teleological argument and St Thomas Aquinas

1 There are no Triggers in this zip file! Find and add in the relevant Triggers.

→

2 Now put the Triggers in the same order as they appear in the AO1 section above.

→

3 Practise 'downloading' your zip file of Triggers from memory. See how many you can recall on first attempt.

↓

6 Now read through your definitions and think about ways in which you could develop these using your Trigger quotes.

←

5 Attempt to write one clear sentence to define each Trigger.

←

4 When you are confident enough, order the Triggers into a list as you may do in an examination situation.

B

ZIP

Paley and Tennant

chance	not understand	beneficial	precise conditions
intelligent mind	human eye	aesthetic	ultimate intelligence
no alternative	planets	no function	infused with beauty
never seen	predictable	nature provides	no survival value
broken	anthropic	sustain life	enquiring

1 Here is your zip file of portable Triggers.

→

2 Practise 'downloading' your zip file of Triggers from memory. See how many you can recall on first attempt.

→

3 When you are confident enough, order the Triggers into a list as you may do in an examination situation.

↓

5 Now read through your descriptions and think about ways in which you could develop these using your Trigger quotes.

←

4 Attempt to write one clear sentence to define each Trigger.

TIP

Why Trigger?
Remember, your Triggers are to help you transfer your knowledge and understanding in a manageable, efficient and portable manner.

AO2 Trigger revision activity

A ZIP

The effectiveness of teleological arguments

1 There are no Triggers in this zip file! Find and add in the relevant Triggers. →

2 Now put the Triggers in the same order as they appear in the AO2 section above. →

3 Practise 'downloading' your zip file of Triggers from memory. See how many you can recall on first attempt.

6 Now read through all your sentences and think about ways in which you could develop these using your Trigger quotes, further examples, and noting strengths and weaknesses. ←

5 Attempt to write one clear sentence to define each Trigger. ←

4 When you are confident enough, order the Triggers into a list as you may do in an examination situation.

B ZIP

The persuasiveness of teleological arguments

alternative explanations	**persuasive today**	**cumulative argument**
advanced information	**inductive**	**Richard Swinburne**
God of the Gaps	**probabilities**	**statistically cumulative force**
cosmological constants	**inexplicable**	**dubious correlations**

1 Here is your zip file of portable Triggers. →

2 Practise 'downloading' your zip file of Triggers from memory. See how many you can recall on first attempt. →

3 When you are confident enough, order the Triggers into a list as you may do in an examination situation.

5 Now read through all your sentences and think about ways in which you could develop these using your Trigger quotes, further examples, and noting strengths and weaknesses. ←

4 'Double-click' each Trigger in your memory – what can you say about an evaluative point of view in a clear sentence? Write this down. Do this for each Trigger in turn. ←

REVISION TIP

Using Trigger quotes
When you choose the Trigger quotes that you wish to use make sure that you explain how they are relevant.

Specification Link

David Hume – empirical objections and critique of causes (cosmological).

AO1

**What is ...
Knowledge and
understanding** ?

This is the skill that involves *selecting* the relevant and appropriate information, *organising* it and then *presenting* it through a *personal explanation* that may involve the use of supporting *evidence* and *examples*.

❛ TRIGGER QUOTES ❜

The concept that every event must have a cause, only applies to the world of sense experience. **(I. Kant)**

… in tracing an eternal succession of objects, it seems absurd to inquire for a general cause or first author. **(D. Hume)**

In such a chain, too, or succession of objects, each part is caused by that which preceded it, and causes that which succeeds it. **(D. Hume)**

Specification Link

David Hume – problems with analogies; rejection of traditional theistic claims: designer not necessarily God of classical theism; apprentice god; plurality of gods; absent god (teleological).

Theme 1C: Challenges to inductive arguments

Hume's objections to the cosmological argument

Hume's objections are directed towards what we infer from causes. His objections are as follows:

- Firstly, Hume sees the idea of looking for a **First Cause** as nonsensical. because he argues that the whole notion of causality is limited to things that begin to exist. If the universe is eternal or infinite, then the question about **cause is irrelevant**:

- Hume also objected to the idea of applying a principle that belonged to a 'part' of the 'whole' equally to the whole itself. This principle has also been developed by Russell who referred to it as the **fallacy of composition**. Just because we observe **cause and effect within** the universe does not mean that this rule applies to the universe collectively and as a **whole**. Hume believed that when we explain every **part** of the universe, we are in fact **explaining the whole** and there is no need to appeal to anything beyond this.

- Finally, Hume argued that we can only reason with certainty the things we have experience of. Since we have **no experience** of creating a universe we therefore cannot talk meaningfully about it. There is not enough empirical **evidence** to argue the universe had a cause and definitely not enough to make any **conclusion** as to what the cause might have been.

Hume's objections to the teleological argument

His objections to the teleological argument are as follows:

- *The analogy is inappropriate.* Hume argued that a scientific view of the universe is very different from a human-made artefact, the world being 'vastly different from ... any object of human experience and observation'. Indeed. the world would appear more **organic** and **not mechanical**.

- *There are other possible analogies*. Hume argued that 'the world plainly resembles more an animal or a vegetable than it does a watch or a knitting loom'. Accordingly,

Scottish Philosopher
David Hume (1711–1776)

he suggested that it would be more consistent to compare the world to a carrot! The **Gaia** hypothesis, put forward in the 1970s by James Lovelock, supports Hume's criticisms; it suggests that earth is a self-regulating, complex interaction between organisms and their inorganic surroundings which work together to contain and maintain life.

- ◼ **The analogy of the watch does not correspond to the** *God of classical theism*. The more the analogy of the man-made machine is emphasised, the more **human God** becomes. The cause ought only to be proportional to the effect, and as the effect is not infinite, so neither have we any reason to ascribe infinity to God.
- ◼ **It makes God similar to an** *apprentice god*. Hume suggests that rather than the Christian God, the analogy is better explained by some **lame performance** by an infant deity, or some inferior and derided deity or even an aged deity!
- ◼ **There could be a** *plurality of gods* **involved**. Hume argued strongly that the world did not closely resemble something made by humans. Shipbuilding is a skill, but one single ship is the 'the result of a process of trial and error' that involves a history of traditions and skills being passed down. Similarly, watchmaking was not a single piece of crafting by one individual.
- ◼ **Analogy leads to a** *non-moral God* **or** *absent God*. Hume pointed out that unpleasant features of nature such as natural disasters and disease raise questions as to the moral character of a God. Hume argued that you cannot attribute to the cause anything more than is sufficient to produce the effect.
- ◼ **There are** *other explanations* **for apparent order**. Hume argued that any universe is bound to have the appearance of design as there could be no universe at all if the parts of it were not mutually adapted to some degree. He makes the distinction between authentic design (deliberate design of an agent) and apparent design (an appearance of design where none actually exists). He refers to the Epicurean hypothesis, which suggests that given time, order will eventually be perceived in the physical world.

Alternative scientific explanations

- ◼ The **Big Bang** theory is often preferred by many as a 'proof' that random action caused by the sudden appearance of a **singularity** (a point in space-time that defies the laws of physics but where infinity exists) can explain the beginning of the universe, not God.
- ◼ In addition, Charles **Darwin** demonstrated that order was not necessarily evidence of purpose and design. The theory of evolution suggests that the combination of **variation and survival** through **natural selection** lead eventually to the emergence of organisms that are suited to their environment. They will have the appearance of design, but the underlying process is more random and unpredictable.
- ◼ Indeed, evolutionary biologist Richard **Dawkins** attacked Paley's argument by pointing out that a true watchmaker has foresight. He designs his cogs and springs and has a future purpose in mind. In contrast, natural selection is blind, unconscious and an automatic process. It is a **blind watchmaker** and God is an unnecessary hypothesis.

⁶**TRIGGER** QUOTES⁹

But the whole, you say, wants a cause. I answer, that the uniting of these parts into a whole, like the uniting of . . . several distinct members into one body, is performed merely by an arbitrary act of the mind ... **(D. Hume)**

The universe is just there, and that is all. **(B. Russell)**

Does not a plant or animal… bear a stronger resemblance to the world, than any artificial machine …? **(D. Hume)**

Quick Revision

Try to identify the distinctive ways in which science challenges both the teleological and the cosmological arguments.

⁶**TRIGGER** QUOTES⁹

All evolutionary biologists know that variation itself is nature's only irreducible essence. **(S. J. Gould)**

The only watchmaker in nature is the blind forces of physics. **(R. Dawkins)**

Specification Link

Alternative scientific explanations including Big Bang theory and Charles Darwin's theory of evolution by natural selection.

Charles Darwin.

Is evolution an adequate alternative to the existence of God?

AO2

What is ...
Evaluation and
critical analysis ?

The AO2 skills of evaluation and critical analysis mean engaging with the controversies surrounding a subject. This is more than merely describing or listing the points made about a controversy. To achieve this, one weighs up strengths and weaknesses of various sides and takes a position. On the right are three controversies for each issue – you can engage in these by extending their arguments (adding examples, quotes or other details), weighing up their strengths and weaknesses, and coming to a conclusion.

❛TRIGGER QUOTES❜

An expanding universe does not preclude a creator, but it does place limits on when he might have carried out his job! **(S. Hawking)**

The analogy between those objects known to proceed from design and any natural object is too weak and too remote to suggest similar causes. **(J. Gaskin)**

Issue:

The effectiveness of the challenges to the cosmological/teleological argument for God's existence

Three evaluative controversies!

☐ **Controversy 1:** *Hume's challenges **to the cosmological logic.***
Hume's challenges to the cosmological argument have been seen by many to be devastating. In particular, the illogical step of actually seeking out a First Cause has been taken up by Russell and others ('The universe is just there, and that is all'). However, Hume's view concerning causes is **not universally accepted**. We distinguish between the ideas of cause and coincidence. This, then, impacts directly upon Hume's first challenge that we ought not to look for a First Cause. Richard **Swinburne** also pointed out that the existence of an observer has no bearing on the **probability** of the occurrence of the events being observed. What needs explaining is the occurrence of the event, not the fact that we have been able to experience the event first hand.

☐ **Controversy 2:** *The watch is a poor analogy for the world.*
The analogies are not precise and Lovelock's **Gaia hypothesis** provides a more appropriate scientific explanation for some. However, some would contend that the **purpose of an analogy** is not is to make a specific point of comparison and the images used cannot be **interpreted rigidly** in every detail. In relation to the conclusion of a being such as God, and then, the implied nature and identity of this being, some would respond by arguing that the design argument is part of a **cumulative argument** and, likewise, the analogy does not claim to demonstrate all the attributes of God in each argument.

☐ **Controversy 3:** *Hume's challenges avoid the obvious conclusions.*
The idea of **several deities** working together can be challenged by **Occam's razor** that, following Swinburne's line of reasoning, asks why we do not draw the **simplest conclusion** and suppose it was one absolute being; the idea of several deities just leads to further questions. What is the major issue here is that both nature and the watch exhibit '**purpose**' and not just design: for many people, purpose **demands an explanation** and some people are not satisfied with the idea that it is 'just there'. Since design and purpose usually suggest intelligence one would need good reason as to why any alternative should be considered.

Sp☉tlight: **Evaluative judgements**

This section contains a special insight that you can use to form a judgement.

Just as the cosmological and teleological arguments themselves may read persuasively until we consider the challenges, then likewise we need to give the challenges an equally rigorous analysis in order to achieve a balanced conclusion.

Issue:

Whether scientific explanations are more persuasive than philosophical explanations for the universe's existence

■ **Controversy 1: *Creation or the Big Bang?***

Modern cosmology suggests that the **Big Bang** implies a finite past history of this universe; evidence that the universe is expanding suggests that it had a starting point (**singularity**). Both science and religion are united on this. Some would argue that there is no external reason; it is just a '**brute fact**' generated by a singularity. Nevertheless, science can **neither prove nor disprove** the existence of God and the idea of a Creator God, for many people, is both an effective answer to the 'big questions' and compatible with a scientific outlook.

■ **Controversy 2: *Darwin's natural selection and the Gaia hypothesis as alternative explanations?***

It could be argued that the work of **Alister McGrath** has clearly demonstrated that **Darwinism** is compatible with conventional religious beliefs and not just with atheism. **Dawkins** contends that science and religion are incompatible. However, science does show how finely tuned the universe is, and one which is conducive to our survival and so for many it would not be inconsistent to suggest God as the explanation of this complex universe. It could be argued that **Lovelock's Gaia hypothesis** would support a more atheistic outlook but like the debate about Big Bang, Lovelock's hypothesis does not rule out a creator God.

■ **Controversy 3: *Are there persuasive alternatives?***

Richard Dawkins completely **rejects religion** so much so that he also aggressively affronts religion. For Dawkins, modern evolutionary theory has no place for God. According to Dawkins, religion involves **infantile** apologetic reasoning but even more dangerously non-thinking and blind acceptance of uninformed ideas that have not been rigorously challenged. Modern evolutionary theory and scientific method have no place for theology. He has even advocated the **meme** as an explanation for non-genetic transfer of cultural, religious and social behaviour. However, some would argue that religious ideas and answers to ultimate questions are **abstract**; they are not physical objects for scientific analysis.

❛TRIGGER QUOTES❜

Curiously, Dawkins and Dennett remain firmly committed to the outmoded notion that science and religion are permanently in conflict. **(A. McGrath)**

God's existence may not be proved … belief in God is eminently reasonable and makes more sense of what we see in the world … **(A. McGrath)**

TIP

The debate about religion and science runs through the WJEC/Eduqas Specification for the World Religions and is at the heart of a modern debate about religious ideas. Why not reflect upon what you have learned in the study of religion to add further insight to your answers.

Alister McGrath is Professor of Divinity and also of Science and Religion in the Faculty of Theology and Religion at Oxford. He also holds a doctorate in Molecular Biophysics!

Sp●tlight: Evaluative judgements

This section contains a special insight that you can use to form a judgement.

The debate about religion and science is at the heart of a modern debate about religious ideas. The relationship is often seen in different ways. Some thinkers reject the significance of religion; however, there is also credibility in seeing religion and science as compatible.

Quick Revision

The controversies have a specific focus but there are areas which intertwine and overlap. Try designing a diagram using your Triggers to map out the various debates involved in the inductive arguments.

AO1 Trigger revision activity

A ZIP

Hume cosmological objections and scientific challenge

First Cause	explaining the whole	singularity	blind watchmaker
cause is irrelevant	no experience	Darwin	
whole	conclusion	natural selection	
part	Big Bang	Dawkins	

1 Fix the zip file! There are four Triggers missing from this zip file – find them and add them in.

→

2 There's another problem: the Triggers are out of order! Put them in the same order as they appear in the AO1 section above.

→

3 Practise 'downloading' your zip file of Triggers from memory. See how many you can recall on first attempt.

↓

6 Now read through your definitions and think about ways in which you could develop these using your Trigger quotes.

←

5 Attempt to write one clear sentence to define each Trigger.

←

4 When you are confident enough, order the Triggers into a list as you may do in an examination situation.

B ZIP

Hume teleological objections

1 There are no Triggers in this zip file! Find and add in the relevant Triggers.

→

2 Now put the Triggers in the same order as they appear in the AO1 section above.

→

3 Practise 'downloading' your zip file of Triggers from memory. See how many you can recall on first attempt.

↓

6 Now read through your definitions and think about ways in which you could develop these using your Trigger quotes.

←

5 Attempt to write one clear sentence to define each Trigger.

←

4 When you are confident enough, order the Triggers into a list as you may do in an examination situation.

AO2 Trigger revision activity

A

ZIP

Effectiveness of the challenges

not universally accepted	purpose of an analogy	Occam's razor
Swinburne	interpreted rigidly	simplest conclusion
probability	several deities	purpose

1 Fix the zip file! There are three Triggers missing from this zip file – find them and add them in. →

2 There's another problem: the Triggers are out of order! Put them in the same order as they appear in the AO2 section above. →

3 Practise 'downloading' your zip file of Triggers from memory. See how many you can recall on first attempt.

6 Now read through all your sentences and think about ways in which you could develop these using your Trigger quotes, further examples, and noting strengths and weaknesses. ←

5 Attempt to write one clear sentence to define each Trigger. ←

4 When you are confident enough, order the Triggers into a list as you may do in an examination situation.

B

ZIP

Scientific or cosmological/teleological

1 There are no Triggers in this zip file! Find and add in the relevant Triggers. →

2 Now put the Triggers in the same order as they appear in the AO2 section above. →

3 Practise 'downloading' your zip file of Triggers from memory. See how many you can recall on first attempt.

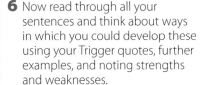

6 Now read through all your sentences and think about ways in which you could develop these using your Trigger quotes, further examples, and noting strengths and weaknesses. ←

5 Attempt to write one clear sentence to define each Trigger. ←

4 When you are confident enough, order the Triggers into a list as you may do in an examination situation.

T2 Deductive arguments

Theme 2A: Origins of the ontological argument

The power and weakness of deduction

Specification Link

Deductive proofs, the concept of a priori.

Spot the Triggers!
The words in blue are Triggers – key words and phrases that can help you remember knowledge and understanding in this area.

TIP

TRIGGER QUOTES

The Greeks... discovered mathematics and the art of deductive reasoning.   **(B. Russell)**

... a single argument which would require no other for its proof than itself alone. **(Anselm)**

'the ontological argument' is best taken as referring to a group of related arguments.
(B. Davies)

The power and weakness of deduction

Before jumping into the **ontological** argument, it's important to recognise that it employs a deductive argument. In a deductive argument, it is impossible for the conclusion to be false if the premises are true. **Deductive** arguments have their own strengths and weaknesses which we examine below.

A priori arguments reach conclusions by considering definitions, ideas and meanings rather than evidence.

Keep in mind that this is different than **inductive** arguments for God; inductive arguments appeal to evidence to support premises. The evidence makes the premises 'probable' so that the conclusion is 'likely'.

Consider this deductive argument:

 + **=**

All plums are fruit   *A prune is a dried plum*   *All prunes are fruit*

Deductive arguments STRONG	Inductive arguments STRONG
If the **premises** are true, you are logically compelled to agree fully with the **conclusion**.	These appeal to experience and facts, so fit our **scientific mindset**.
You don't need to work finding experiences and facts to back up the conclusion! (**a priori** – without or prior to evidence)	Premises appeal to evidence (**a posteriori**). The more evidence, the more compelling the conclusion.
Deductive arguments WEAK	**Inductive arguments WEAK**
The deductive argument fails if a **premise is weak**.	It can take **a lot of work** to find evidence!
If premises don't **fit with facts** we experience, we might not be convinced!	You **never get 100%** there. Even Dawkins can't reach absolute certainty: there is 'probably no God'.

Anselm's Proslogion 2 and 3

Anselm **B**ases **C**hristianity on Faith.

(But he believes his **faith** will help him find irresistible **reasons** to believe.)

Proslogion 2: **God by a single argument**

The essential points:
- This argument assumes this **definition of God**: 'a being than which nothing greater can be conceived'.
- This argument can be **summarised** in this way:
- PREMISE 1: It is possible to exist both in the mind and/or in reality.
- PREMISE 2: It is greater to **exist in reality** than only in the **mind alone**.
- CONCLUSION: If God is as we have defined, then **God must exist** both in the mind and in reality.

Proslogion 3: **Anselm develops the argument**

Contingency and necessity
Below are several images. We would say that these have '**contingent** existence'. By this we mean that their existence is dependent on other things. As we come to Anselm's development of the ontological argument, it is important to know the difference between contingent existence (the items below) and 'necessary existence'. Necessary existence is defined below – it refers to something that does not have contingent existence.

Another form of the ontological argument
Anselm believes God has the quality of **necessary** existence: by which he means that God, unlike the items pictured above, cannot be thought of as not existing. Necessary existence is a unique feature; no objects we see in our everyday lives possess it. This idea leads to another form of the argument. Here is one way to express it:

- PREMISE 1: Necessary existence is greater than contingent existence.
- PREMISE 2: It is possible to think of a being that has necessary existence (a being that must exist).
- PREMISE 3: God's existence can either be necessary or contingent.
- CONCLUSION: Given that God is a being than which nothing greater can be conceived, God's existence is necessary.

Specification Link

St Anselm – God as the greatest possible being (Proslogion 2). St Anselm – God has necessary existence (Proslogion 3).

❝TRIGGER QUOTES❞

I believe in order to understand. **(Anselm)**

God: 'a being than which nothing greater can be conceived'. **(Anselm)**

Quick Revision

Write out one simple argument that uses induction and one simple argument that uses deduction – these do not need to reference God or religion. Then, make a list of the strengths and weaknesses of each argument. You can use this list to prepare for an examination question asking for an evaluation of inductive and deductive approaches.

Issue:

The extent to which 'a priori' arguments for God's existence are persuasive

Three evaluative controversies!

- **Controversy 1:** *A priori arguments are persuasive because of their elegant simplicity!*
  They require only an understanding of language and not the **hard work of gathering evidence**. They also do not rest on the constantly shifting interpretations that can be made when using evidence. However, though a priori arguments have an elegant simplicity, it is simple for them to **fail**. If a premise is suspect, inaccurate or wrong in an a priori argument, the entire argument fails. A posteriori reasoning is stronger because the premise doesn't need to be convincing alone, it can be '**probable**'; many 'probables' add up to a 'likely true'. This can be seen as a better foundation for knowledge than a priori reasoning.

- **Controversy 2:** *A priori arguments have inescapable conclusions!*
  This is because the conclusion states what is known and is accepted in the premises. If one **follows the premises**, then one must accept a conclusion which is founded on those premises. However, **legitimate questions** can be raised for many of the premises of the ontological argument. For example, the premise that it is greater to exist in reality than to exist in the mind alone can be challenged by the universal human activity of creating and enjoying myths. As soon as just one legitimate question arises, then the **argument falls apart**.

- **Controversy 3:** *The ontological argument remains compelling throughout the world!*
  Anselm formulated this argument nearly **1000 years** ago and philosophers of religion are still discussing it. Perhaps this is because it is a nearly **universal conviction** that there must be some 'ultimate reality' underlying existence. If this is the case, one might consider that this reality can be discovered 'a priori', outside of needing evidence. However, that something 'nearly universally' believed must be true does not satisfy the 21st-century mind. An a priori argument gives **no evidence** outside of the language it uses. Correspondences between language, meaning and ideas can never guarantee the existence of anything.

AO2

What is ... Evaluation and critical analysis **?**

The AO2 skills of evaluation and critical analysis mean engaging with the controversies surrounding a subject. This is more than merely describing or listing the points made about a controversy. To achieve this, one weighs up strengths and weaknesses of various sides and takes a position. On the right are three controversies for each issue – you can engage in these by extending their arguments (adding examples, quotes or other details), weighing up their strengths and weaknesses, and coming to a conclusion.

❝TRIGGER QUOTES❞

An expanding universe does not preclude a creator, but it does place limits on when he might have carried out his job! **(S. Hawking)**

The analogy between those objects known to proceed from design and any natural object is too weak and too remote to suggest similar causes. **(Gaskin)**

Quick Revision

For each of the bullet-point-premises from Proslogion 2 and 3, write down (i) the meaning of this premise in your own words and (ii) whether or not you agree or disagree with that premise – and why. This will help you in an exam evaluation question on the ontological argument.

Spotlight: Evaluative judgements

This section contains a special insight that you can use to form a judgement.

Can any of these premises be questioned? If so, include your views on this to expand the controversies above.

from Proslogion 2:
- It is possible to exist both in the mind and/or in reality.
- It is greater to exist in reality than only in the mind alone.

from Proslogion 3:
- Necessary existence is greater than contingent existence.
- It is possible to think of a being that has necessary existence (a being that must exist).
- Everything other than God has a contingent existence.

Issue:

The extent to which different religious views on the nature of God impact on arguments for the existence of God

- ▣ **Controversy 1:** *Arguments for God's existence are greatly impacted by beliefs about God's nature.*

  The various arguments for God (cosmological, teleological and ontological) arise from **classical theism**, by those who participate in the **Abrahamic religions** and who are united by belief that the nature of God is **omnipotent**, omniscient and omnipresent. Indeed, the cosmological and teleological arguments presume that God is powerful enough to create a universe and the ontological presumes that God possesses perfection. However, there are many key aspects believed about the nature of God that are not reflected by these arguments; for instance, God's omnibenevolence. These arguments could even be seen to be 'true' with a malevolent or passive deity.

- ▣ **Controversy 2:** *Arguments for the existence of God take place in a theoretical vacuum!*

  These arguments are a rational exercise which focuses on the relationship of language, meaning and ideas to **universal concepts** of evidence and logic. As such, they have not been impacted at all by specific religious belief. In fact, most believers from the Abrahamic traditions would say that one cannot grasp God's nature without **specific revelation**. However, Anselm would say that there is a relationship between faith and reason (**faith seeking reason**) and many theologians would say that there is a relationship between 'general' and 'specific' revelation; arguments for God reflect the God of general revelation.

- ▣ **Controversy 3:** *Arguments for God's existence are moderately impacted by faith in God's nature.*

  These arguments arise from specific **theological** contexts – they are not the result of Buddhist thinking in which 'God' or 'Gods' are a lesser reality and not necessary for the attaining of enlightenment. This means that they are accompanied by '**theistic baggage**' which includes many (but not all) ideas about God found in Christianity, Judaism and Islam. However, the fact that these arguments have had an **appeal outside of these religions** shows that they may contain the universal ideas and appeal to those outside of monotheistic faiths.

Sp🔴tlight: Evaluative judgements

This section contains a special insight that you can use to form a judgement.

In the Abrahamic religions, revealed theology comes from the sacred texts which demonstrate much more than the fact of God's existence; they reveal the character of God to be loving, just, wise – and many other qualities. For instance, the famous Muslim theologian Al-Ghazali wrote a book entitled 'The 99 Beautiful Names of God'. Many theologians from these religions also believe in 'natural theology' – that something of God's nature can be known outside of special revelation.

Arguments for God could be compatible with an evil being!

AO1 Trigger revision activity

A
ZIP

The power and weakness of deduction

ontological	premises	premise is weak	a posteriori
deductive	conclusion	fit with facts	a lot of work
inductive	a priori	scientific mindset	never get 100%

1 Here is your zip file of portable Triggers.

2 Practise 'downloading' your zip file of Triggers from memory. See how many you can recall on first attempt.

3 When you are confident enough, order the Triggers into a list as you may do in an examination situation.

Why Trigger?
Remember, your Triggers are to help you transfer your knowledge and understanding in a manageable, efficient and portable manner.

TIP

5 Now read through your descriptions and think about ways in which you could develop these using your Trigger quotes.

4 Attempt to write one clear sentence to define each Trigger.

B
ZIP

Proslogion 2 and 3

definition of God	exist in reality
faith	necessary
Proslogion 2	God must exist
ABC	contingent
summarised	Mind alone

1 Fix the zip file! There are two Triggers missing from this zip file – find them and add them in.

2 There's another problem: the Triggers are out of order! Put them in the same order as they appear in the AO1 section above.

3 Practise 'downloading' your zip file of Triggers from memory. See how many you can recall on first attempt.

6 Now read through your definitions and think about ways in which you could develop these using your Trigger quotes.

5 Attempt to write one clear sentence to define each Trigger.

4 When you are confident enough, order the Triggers into a list as you may do in an examination situation.

AO2 Trigger revision activity

A ZIP

A priori as persuasive

elegant simplicity! hard work of gathering evidence, fail, probable	inescapable conclusions! follows the premises, legitimate questions, argument falls apart	compelling! 1000 years, universal conviction, no evidence

1 Here is your zip file of portable Triggers.

2 Practise 'downloading' your zip file of Triggers from memory. See how many you can recall on first attempt.

3 When you are confident enough, order the Triggers into a list as you may do in an examination situation.

5 Now read through all your sentences and think about ways in which you could develop these using your Trigger quotes, further examples, and noting strengths and weaknesses.

4 'Double-click' each Trigger in your memory – what can you say about an evaluative point of view in a clear sentence? Write this down. Do this for each Trigger in turn.

REVISION TIP

Using Trigger quotes
When you choose the Trigger quotes that you wish to use, make sure that you explain how they are relevant.

B ZIP

Nature of God and arguments for God

moderately impacted, theological, appeal outside of these religions	theoretical vacuum! universal concepts, specific revelation	greatly impacted, Abrahamic religions, omnipotent

1 Fix the zip file! There are three Triggers missing from this zip file – find them and add them in.

2 There's another problem: the Triggers are out of order! Put them in the same order as they appear in the AO2 section above.

3 Practise 'downloading' your zip file of Triggers from memory. See how many you can recall on first attempt.

6 Now read through all your sentences and think about ways in which you could develop these using your Trigger quotes, further examples, and noting strengths and weaknesses.

5 Attempt to write one clear sentence to define each Trigger.

4 When you are confident enough, order the Triggers into a list as you may do in an examination situation.

T2 Deductive arguments

Theme 2B: **Developments of the ontological argument**

Rene Descartes

Specification **Link**

Rene Descartes – concept of God as supremely perfect being; analogies of triangles and mountains/valleys.

Ever wanted to achieve a perfect score? Descartes defines God as a 'supremely perfect being'.

AO1

What is ...
Knowledge and
understanding ■ **?**

This is the skill that involves *selecting* the relevant and appropriate information, *organising* it and then *presenting* it through a *personal explanation* that may involve the use of supporting *evidence* and *examples*.

Spot the Triggers!
The words in blue are Triggers – key words and phrases that can help you remember knowledge and understanding in this area. **TIP**

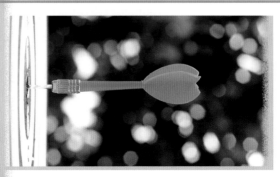

- ■ Descartes says that just as one can have a **clear idea** of numbers, one can have a clear idea of God.
- ■ Anselm's definition of God used a negative (that-than-which-nothing-greater-can-be-conceived); Descartes begins with a positive: 'a **supremely perfect being**'.
- ■ Classical theism discusses **attributes** such as power (omnipotence), knowledge (omniscience) and love (omnibenevolence) in relation to God – Descartes includes existence.
- ■ **Existence** is one of the many perfections or attributes of God.
- ■ **Analogy 1: triangle** – existence goes with God just as angles go with a triangle.
- ■ **Analogy 2: mountains** – existence belongs with God just as valleys belong with mountains.
- ■ In order to think about triangles and mountains, one must use a set of **criteria** or attributes – this is no different than God.
- ■ Attributes are a **necessary** aspect of any definition.
- ■ Existence is **inseparable** from God
- ■ God alone possesses this perfection or attribute of **necessary existence**.
- ■ The assumption behind Descartes' approach is that existence is a 'property' or a '**predicate**'.

6 *TRIGGER* QUOTES 9

The second main period in the history of the ontological argument begins with Rene Descartes ...   (J. Hick)

... the idea of God ... is one which I find within me just as surely as the idea of any shape or number.   (R. Descartes)

I cannot think of God except as existing, just as I cannot think of a mountain without a valley.   (R. Descartes)

Each of Descartes' analogies can be found in this image. Can you find them?

Norman Malcolm

- Norman Malcolm is in favour of the ontological argument, though he **rejects** Anselm's Proslogion 2 as well as Descartes' view of existence as a perfection.
- He sides with **Gaunilo and Kant** against them: you can't just add existence to an object's list of qualities and then declare that object to exist!
- Existence is **not a perfection**; it does not make something 'better' than it had been without it.
- An '**insulated house**', Malcolm says, is better than an 'uninsulated house'. However, it does not make sense to say that an 'existing house' is better than a 'non-existing house'.
- Malcolm believes, with Anselm in Proslogion 3, that **necessary existence** follows from the notion of that-than-which-nothing-greater-can-be-conceived.
- This is because it is **absurd** to believe in a *that-than-which-nothing-greater-can-be-thought* that does not exist.
- A being that did not have necessary existence would be **inferior** to a being that necessarily existed.
- This greatest possible being which has necessary existence can be described as an **unlimited being**, a being that has no limits.
- If God were limited in any way, then God would not be that-than-which-nothing-greater-can-be-conceived and therefore not be worthy of **worship**.

An Argument from Malcolm

Malcolm explores why God's existence is necessary. This can be represented in a deductive argument – though Malcolm did not represent it in this exact way:

Premise 1	The definition of God as that-than-which-nothing-greater-can-be-conceived is a **logically sound description** of an unlimited, necessarily existing being.
Premise 2	An unlimited being **cannot come into existence**, for this would mean that he was caused to exist or just happened to exist – each qualities of limited beings.
Premise 3	An unlimited being **cannot cease existing**, as ceasing to exist is a quality of a limited being.
Conclusion	Therefore, God's existence is either **impossible or necessary**. Since it would only be impossible if the definition in Premise 1 were logically flawed, it follows that God necessarily exists.

Specification Link

Norman Malcolm – God as unlimited being: God's existence as necessary rather than just possible.

❝ TRIGGER QUOTES ❞

His existence must either be logically necessary or logically impossible.

(N. Malcolm)

Malcolm is thinking of something which does not depend for its existence on anything apart from itself. **(B. Davies)**

Quick Revision

In your own words, express what Malcolm accepts and does not accept from the arguments of Anselm and Descartes. This will help you with any exam questions both on Malcolm and on the ontological argument.

Malcolm, Gaunilo and Kant: you cannot simply add existence to an object's list of qualities and then declare that it exists.

What is ...
Evaluation and
critical analysis ?

The AO2 skills of evaluation and critical analysis mean engaging with the controversies surrounding a subject. This is more than merely describing or listing the points made about a controversy. To achieve this, one weighs up strengths and weaknesses of various sides and takes a position. On the right are three controversies for each issue – you can engage in these by extending their arguments (adding examples, quotes or other details), weighing up their strengths and weaknesses, and coming to a conclusion.

Issue:
The effectiveness of the ontological argument for God's existence

Three evaluative controversies!

- **Controversy 1:** *It comes with the strengths of an a priori argument!*
  As a rational proof, the ontological argument 'works': it presents a conclusion which is **inescapable** given the acceptance of the premises. This is why it has gained the attention of **great minds** over hundreds of years from Anselm to Descartes and Malcolm. However, the **Achilles' heel** of an a priori argument is the weakness of any one of the premises. In the case of the ontological argument, any one of the premises can be shown to be weak. For instance, it could be argued that Anselm's notion that something existing in both the mind and reality is greater than that which exists only in the mind is a presupposition rather than obviously true.

- **Controversy 2:** *It has an appeal outside of religion!*
  Descartes begins his reflection on God as a purely **conceptual enterprise**, which he compares to meditating on numbers or other intellectual ideas. He builds his argument using notions such as perfections and attributes, arguing that just as any object is inseparable from certain attributes, so is God inseparable from the **attribute of existence**. However, it must not be forgotten that Descartes was a devout Catholic – and those who used this argument were similarly committed to their faith. This means that this argument can be seen as building upon a **religious foundation** rather than establishing it.

- **Controversy 3:** *It has been developed to meet objections!*
  A strength of any theory is its ability to adapt in the face of objections; this is precisely the case with **Malcolm's defense** of the theory, when he agrees with critics (Gaunilo and Kant) of Proslogion 2 and their objections to defining a concept into existence. Malcolm shows the relevance of Anselm's concept of '**necessary existence**', adapting this into a revised argument that shows how the existence of an unlimited being is either impossible or necessary. Yet this has not even convinced some religious believers! For instance, John Hick says that Malcolm's 'logical necessity' and 'logical impossibility' are **hypothetical** – IF God exists eternally, then what Malcolm says is true. However, this does not mean that God exists.

Sp●tlight: **Evaluative judgements**
This section contains a special insight that you can use to form a judgement.

Beware of an argument that appeals to authority (the 'argumentum ad verecundiam') in relation to the ontological argument. This is an argument which urges a certain viewpoint because other 'great' people agree with it or the viewpoint has a time-honoured history. These kinds of argument are irrelevant as 'great' people have been wrong and some theories (such as a flat earth) have a long history but are false.

Issue:

Whether the ontological argument is more persuasive than the cosmological/teleological arguments for God's existence

- **Controversy 1:** *It depends on the status of a priori arguments!*

  If one is willing to accept an a priori **deductive approach** when it comes to proofs for God's existence, then one might see the strengths of this approach, with its **inescapable conclusion**, as greater than inductive approaches, which depend on the accumulation of evidence that is never fully certain. However, a deductive approach has a low status in our contemporary world in which **scientific advancement** is based on empirical methods which seek to establish evidence for theories. Proponents of the cosmological and teleological arguments, such as William Lane Craig, can appeal to a scientific mindset as they seek to show that God is the most 'probable' explanation for the evidence that we see around us.

- **Controversy 2:** *The foundations of cosmological/teleological arguments are more certain.*

  Whilst the ontological argument can be dismissed as 'hypothetical' at best or a 'word game' at worst, there is little doubt that the foundations of the cosmological and teleological arguments are widely recognised: we do **observe** the universe and live in an ordered and purposeful world. These arguments proceed to explain these **universal truths**. However, these observations are not as straightforward as they appear. For, as we have no knowledge of a non-universe-existence, the observation of the existence of a universe is meaningless. Furthermore, the observation that the world is ordered and purposeful is entirely **subjective** as arguments for chaos can be made to explain away apparent 'order'.

- **Controversy 3:** *Both ways fail equally to prove 'God'.*

  These arguments fail to bring one to the God that is worshipped by the proponents of those arguments, namely, the God of the Abrahamic faiths. This is because, as David Hume has pointed out, there is no content for the **character of God** produced other than omnipotence or omniscience. The 'God' produced by these arguments could be a malevolent deity, a passive and uninvolved force, or even a group of **advanced aliens** who 'seeded' our planet long ago. Yet, this criticism fails to appreciate the context of these arguments, which is not to convince unbelievers but to show believers that there is a relationship between **faith and reason** – 'faith seeking understanding' (Anselm).

❝ *TRIGGER* QUOTES ❞

Recent developments in astronomical and cosmological theory have emphasised the mysteriousness of the universe ... **(J. Hick)**

You forget, that this superlative intelligence and benevolence are entirely imaginary. **(D. Hume)**

Scientifically speaking, it is far more probable for a life-prohibiting universe to exist than a life-sustaining one. **(W. L. Craig)**

TIP

When you use Trigger Quotes in an exam response, make sure that you explain how they are relevant.

Quick Revision

In your own words, explain the two Trigger quotes by Hick in this evaluation section. Then, write down a few reasons that could be used to support both (i) the idea of ontological argument fitting with the fact of mystery and (ii) how it oversimplifies the fact of mystery. This will help you with an exam evaluation question on the persuasiveness of the ontological argument.

Sp💡tlight: Evaluative judgements

This section contains a special insight that you can use to form a judgement.

Instead of clear answers to the origin and meaning of this complex cosmos, there is a mystery. We do not know, for example, if the Big Bang was an absolute beginning or one of an endless series of Big Bang events. This mystery can be used either to show the foolishness of a religious proof about God – or it can be used to show that there is indeed room for a religious response since science itself has no final answer to the origin of the universe.

An argument from authority attempts to persuade because 'important' people agree, or the argument has a long, distinguished history.

AO1 Trigger revision activity

A
ZIP

Descartes' ontological argument

1 There are no Triggers in this zip file! Find and add in the relevant Triggers.

2 Now put the Triggers in the same order as they appear in the AO1 section above.

3 Practise 'downloading' your zip file of Triggers from memory. See how many you can recall on first attempt.

6 Now read through your definitions and think about ways in which you could develop these using your Trigger quotes.

5 Attempt to write one clear sentence to define each Trigger.

4 When you are confident enough, order the Triggers into a list as you may do in an examination situation.

B
ZIP

Norman Malcolm

rejects	insulated house	matrix	cannot come into existence
Gaunilo and Kant	necessary existence	unlimited being	cannot cease existing
in floor heating	absurd	worship	Vulcan
		cacophony	

1 Find the unhelpful Triggers! **This zip file contains several inappropriate or irrelevant Triggers**. Find these and replace them with the real Triggers from the AO1 section.

2 There's another problem: the Triggers are out of order! Put them in the same order as they appear in the AO1 section above.

3 Practise 'downloading' your zip file of Triggers from memory. See how many you can recall on first attempt.

6 Now read through your definitions and think about ways in which you could develop these using your Trigger quotes.

5 Attempt to write one clear sentence to define each Trigger.

4 When you are confident enough, order the Triggers into a list as you may do in an examination situation.

AO2 Trigger revision activity

A ZIP

Effectiveness of ontological arguments

1 There are no Triggers in this zip file! Find and add in the relevant Triggers. **→**

2 Now put the Triggers in the same order as they appear in the AO2 section above. **→**

3 Practise 'downloading' your zip file of Triggers from memory. See how many you can recall on first attempt.

↓

6 Now read through all your sentences and think about ways in which you could develop these using your Trigger quotes, further examples, and noting strengths and weaknesses. **←**

5 Attempt to write one clear sentence to define each Trigger. **←**

4 When you are confident enough, order the Triggers into a list as you may do in an examination situation.

B ZIP

Ontological vs. Teleological/Cosmological

Fail equally, character of God, reptiles, faith & reason	**Foundations more certain, observe, universal studios, subjective**	**Status of a priori arguments! S. Holmes, inescapable conclusion, higher maths**

1 Find the unhelpful Triggers! **This zip file contains several inappropriate or irrelevant Triggers**. Find these and replace them with the real Triggers from the AO2 section. **→**

2 There's another problem: the Triggers are out of order! Put them in the same order as they appear in the AO2 section above. **→**

3 Practise 'downloading' your zip file of Triggers from memory. See how many you can recall on first attempt.

↓

6 Now read through all your sentences and think about ways in which you could develop these using your Trigger quotes, further examples, and noting strengths and weaknesses. **←**

5 Attempt to write one clear sentence to define each Trigger. **←**

4 When you are confident enough, order the Triggers into a list as you may do in an examination situation.

Specification Link

Gaunilo, his reply to St Anselm; his rejection of the idea of a greatest possible being that can be thought of as having separate existence outside of our minds; his analogy of the idea of the greatest island as a ridicule of St Anselm's logic.

AO1

What is ... Knowledge and understanding ?

This is the skill that involves *selecting* the relevant and appropriate information, *organising* it and then *presenting* it through a *personal explanation* that may involve the use of supporting *evidence* and *examples*.

Spot the Triggers!

The words in blue are Triggers – key words and phrases that can help you remember knowledge and understanding in this area.

TIP

6 *TRIGGER* QUOTES 9

I know nothing at all of the latter [Anselm's definition of God] save for the verbal formula. **(Gaunilo)**

According to Gaunilo, if Anselm is correct then it is not only God's existence that can be established by reasoning akin to Anselm's. **(B. Davies)**

You cannot ... doubt that this island that is more excellent than any other lands truly exists ... **(Gaunilo's reduction of Anselm's argument)**

We would say that this is an 'absurd' picture because giraffes do not climb trees. Gaunilo shows that Anselm's argument is absurd because 'most excellent' islands do not necessarily exist.

Theme 2C: **Challenges to the ontological argument**

Gaunilo's reply to Anselm

- Gaunilo, a contemporary of Anselm, was a **monk** in France.
- He entitled his reply to Anselm, 'On behalf of the **fool**', a reference to Anselm's view that a fool who does not believe in God could be refuted.
- Gaunilo first says that Anselm's definition of God **cannot be understood** in the mind as it is unlike any other understanding we possess.
- The 'fool' would only hear Anselm's definition as **mere words** rather than as truth – unless God had assisted this understanding.
- Then, Gaunilo attempts to show how Anselm's argument is absurd by **substituting an island** for God.
- Anselm had claimed that God (defined as 'that-than-which-nothing-greater-can-be-conceived') must exist, as it is **greater to exist** than to not exist.

- Gaunilo asks us to imagine the **most excellent island**, though it would have been better if he had used 'an island than which no greater island can be conceived'.
- His main point is that just because you can think of a 'most excellent island', it would be a **logical nonsense** to conclude that it must exist.
- Gaunilo's approach is known as a '**reductio ad absurdum**'; this is an argument that highlights the absurdity of a conclusion when followed by seemingly sound premises.

- Anselm responded to Gaunilo, saying that the ontological argument applies only to God; an 'island' simply **cannot be compared** with 'God'.
- In Proslogion 3 Anslem had noted the difference between **contingent and necessary** existence; an island is contingent, dependent on the natural world.
- Critics of Gaunilo have pointed out that his island contains no **intrinsic maximum** – that is, it can always be added to and improved.
- A non-contingent God has an intrinsic maximum; that is, **perfection** is a necessary part of God.

Kant argues that 'existence' adds nothing to one's concept of God.

Immanuel Kant's criticisms

- Immanuel Kant was an **18th-century** Prussian philosopher who criticised Descartes' form of the ontological argument.
- **Critique 1: hypothetical**. If Descartes says, 'if there is a God', then a hypothetical God exists – it is possible for 'God' to be a hypothetical necessity. However, to say that 'God exists necessarily' is not hypothetical; it is a judgement that **needs proof**.
- This is the same with **angles within a triangle** – they logically belong together; however, this fact does not prove that there are triangles!
- **Critique 2: predicates**. Existence is not a predicate because it tells us nothing about the nature of an object. A predicate is a **defining characteristic** or an attribute; for example, in the statement 'God is omnipotent', the predicate omnipotence tells us something about the character of God. However, in the statement 'God exists', the predicate exists **tells one nothing** about the character of God.
- A 100 real **thalers** (a currency used in Kant's day) does not contain any more coins than 100 imaginary thalers.
- There is **no meaningful addition** to our understanding of the nature of a subject when we say it 'exists'.

TRIGGER QUOTES

To posit a triangle, and yet to reject its three angles, is self-contradictory; but there is no contradiction in rejecting the triangle together with its three angles. **(I. Kant)**

... a determining predicate is a predicate which is added to the concept of the subject and enlarges it. **(I. Kant)**

'Being' is obviously not a real predicate. **(I. Kant)**

Quick Revision

Write down two ways that Gaunilo 'scores' against Anselm. Write down two ways in which Gaunilo fails to 'score'. This will help you on an exam question asking you to describe challenges to the ontological argument.

TIP

Remember, your Triggers are to help you transfer your knowledge and understanding in a manageable, efficient and portable manner.

What is ...
Evaluation and
critical analysis ?

The AO2 skills of evaluation and critical analysis mean engaging with the controversies surrounding a subject. This is more than merely describing or listing the points made about a controversy. To achieve this, one weighs up strengths and weaknesses of various sides and takes a position. On the right are three controversies for each issue – you can engage in these by extending their arguments (adding examples, quotes or other details), weighing up their strengths and weaknesses, and coming to a conclusion.

Issue:
The effectiveness of the challenges to the ontological argument for God's existence

Three evaluative controversies!

- **Controversy 1: *Gaunilo's challenge strikes at the core!***
Anselm's argument that God exists rests on **two central ideas**: (i) God defined as that-than-which-nothing-greater-can-be-conceived and (ii) existing in reality and in the mind is greater than existing in the mind alone – Anselm viewed these two ideas working together to prove the existence of God. By **substituting** 'the most excellent island' (or any other object) for God, Gaunilo showed that Anselm's approach could be used to show that almost anything perfect could exist and that therefore it was weak at the core. However, Gaunilo has missed the core of Anselm's argument of **Proslogion 3** which is that no substitutions can be made as God alone has necessary existence – an island merely has contingent existence.

- **Controversy 2: *Kant's challenge reveals empty words!***
Descartes had tried to say that God, defined as a being with **all perfections** included the perfection (or attribute) of existence. However, Kant showed that perfections are predicates which tell us something new about a concept – 'existence' adds **nothing new** to one's understanding of a concept and it is therefore not a predicate. For example, a 'red car' tells us something about a car, but an 'existing car' adds nothing to our understanding of a car. Yet, is not Descartes right to suggest that **a non-existing God** is very different than an existing God and that therefore existence tells us something meaningful about God?

- **Controversy 3: *Both Gaunilo and Kant work with* concepts that we know!**
The reason that Gaunilo and Kant provide effective challenges to the ontological argument is that they seek to **apply this argument** to concepts and objects that are **familiar** to us: islands and descriptions of concepts that we use every day (i.e. 100 thalers). However, can't we accept that fact that there is at least one concept (God) that is **unique**? Thus, a failure to apply what we know in the 'real' world does not mean that God does not exist. We must see, as did Anselm and Descartes, that God is in a category all by Him-Her-Itself.

⟨ *TRIGGER* QUOTES ⟩

Existence is not a predicate in that [Anslem's] sense, and any argument which presupposes that it is must be an invalid argument.
(J. Hick)

... the famous ontological argument of Descartes is therefore merely so much labour and effort lost ...
(I. Kant)

Sp⬤tlight: **Evaluative judgements**
This section contains a special insight that you can use to form a judgement.

Gaunilo applied Anselm's definition 'that-than-which-nothing-greater-can-be conceived' to 'the most excellent island'. However, this misses the fact that Anselm never said the 'most excellent God' or that God was greater than anything else. Therefore, Gaunilo starts on the 'wrong foot'. However, Gaunilo's argument can be adapted to make a better challenge to Anselm: 'an island than which no island greater can be conceived'.

Issue:

The extent to which objections to the ontological argument are persuasive

- ◩ **Controversy 1: *Gaunilo shows Anselm's absurdity!***

  Gaunilo's strategy is effective as it promises to **test** the relationship of Anselm's premises to his conclusion. It succeeds because it points to the possibility that Anselm may be simply defining God into existence, when other impossible things can similarly be defined into existence. However, Gaunilo simply does not make an **accurate substitution**: a 'most excellent island' is not equivalent to that-than-which-nothing-greater can be conceived. Furthermore, even if he were to make an equivalent substitution, Anselm would argue that God is a necessary being whereas the island always remains a **contingent reality**.

- ◩ **Controversy 2: *Kant shows the ontological argument is masking assertions as proofs!***

  Kant notes that it is entirely logical to argue that certain **concepts belong** to one another (as angles to a triangle); however, this assertion does not mean that the concepts discussed actually exist. Furthermore, he notes that 'existence' **adds nothing** to understanding a concept as predicates normally do. Therefore 'a most excellent being' cannot include the attribute/perfection/quality of existence since it is not a predicate. However, some believe that the intention of the ontological argument is not so much to prove God's existence but to **enrich** the Christian understanding of God as the highest possible reality. In this, it is successful, though this argument appeals to only a limited audience.

- ◩ **Controversy 3: *There are just too many questions to make the ontological argument persuasive.***

  There are a number of questions which warn one away from accepting the ontological argument. For example, is it not true that **existence implies limitation**? After all, we know that everything that does exist has limitations. This seems to rule out God existing. Also, wouldn't an 'unlimited being' be indistinguishable from 'non-being'? Finally, are the perfections of God really compatible if they are **multiplied to infinity**? For example, how can God be both 100% just and 100% merciful? These questions could be countered by arguing that we are bound to run into questions given our finite nature. This does not mean that our **intuition of infinite** reality is wrong.

Gaunilo tests Anselm's argument by substituting a 'most excellent island' for 'God'.

Quick Revision

In your own words, explain the two Trigger quotes by Hick in this evaluation section. Then, write down how a few reasons that could be used to support both (i) the idea of ontological argument fitting with the fact of mystery and (ii) how it oversimplifies the fact of mystery. This will help you with an exam evaluation question on the persuasiveness of the ontological argument.

❝TRIGGER QUOTES❞

If the idea of the greatest possible island is incoherent, must not the same be true of the greatest possible being? **(B. Davies)**

When therefore, I think a being as the supreme reality, without any defect, the question still remains whether it exists or not. **(I. Kant)**

A definition of God describes one's concept of God but cannot prove the actual existence of any such being. **(J. Hick)**

Sp⬤tlight: Evaluative judgements

This section contains a special insight that you can use to form a judgement.

Immanuel Kant discussed the difference between analytic and synthetic statements. An analytic statement is true simply by definition. Here is an example: 'all oculists are eye doctors'. This is also known as a tautology, saying the same thing twice using different words. It is possible to define God to include existence – this, he says, is merely an analytic statement, nothing but a 'miserable tautology'. However, synthetic statements are true not by definition alone, but have a relationship to the world of sense perception. Descartes does not make a synthetic assertion in this argument according to Kant.

AO1 Trigger revision activity

A ZIP

Gaunilo

greater to exist	**mere words**	**reductio ad absurdum**
fool	**substituting an island**	**cannot be compared**
cannot be understood	**contingent and necessary**	**most excellent island**
	perfection	**logical nonsense**

1 Fix the zip file! There are two Triggers missing from this zip file – find them and add them in.

2 There's another problem: the Triggers are out of order! Put them in the same order as they appear in the AO1 section above.

3 Practise 'downloading' your zip file of Triggers from memory. See how many you can recall on first attempt.

4 When you are confident enough, order the Triggers into a list as you may do in an examination situation.

5 Attempt to write one clear sentence to define each Trigger.

6 Now read through your definitions and think about ways in which you could develop these using your Trigger quotes.

B ZIP

Kant's objections

1 There are no Triggers in this zip file! Find and add in the relevant Triggers.

2 Now put the Triggers in the same order as they appear in the AO1 section above.

3 Practise 'downloading' your zip file of Triggers from memory. See how many you can recall on first attempt.

4 When you are confident enough, order the Triggers into a list as you may do in an examination situation.

5 Attempt to write one clear sentence to define each Trigger.

6 Now read through your definitions and think about ways in which you could develop these using your Trigger quotes.

AO2 Trigger revision activity

A ZIP

Effective challenges: ontological argument

concepts that we know!	Kant's challenge	Gaunilo's challenge
apply this argument	all perfections	two central ideas
unique	a non-existing God	substituting

1 Fix the zip file! There are three Triggers missing from this zip file – find them and add them in.

2 There's another problem: the Triggers are out of order! Put them in the same order as they appear in the AO2 section above.

3 Practise 'downloading' your zip file of Triggers from memory. See how many you can recall on first attempt.

4 When you are confident enough, order the Triggers into a list as you may do in an examination situation.

5 Attempt to write one clear sentence to define each Trigger.

6 Now read through all your sentences and think about ways in which you could develop these using your Trigger quotes, further examples, and noting strengths and weaknesses.

B ZIP

Ontological argument persuasiveness

1 There are no Triggers in this zip file! Find and add in the relevant Triggers.

2 Now put the Triggers in the same order as they appear in the AO2 section above.

3 Practise 'downloading' your zip file of Triggers from memory. See how many you can recall on first attempt.

4 When you are confident enough, order the Triggers into a list as you may do in an examination situation.

5 Attempt to write one clear sentence to define each Trigger.

6 Now read through all your sentences and think about ways in which you could develop these using your Trigger quotes, further examples, and noting strengths and weaknesses.

Challenges to religious belief – the problem of evil and suffering

Theme 3A: The problem of evil and suffering

The types of evil

Within theological debate about the problem of evil two different types of evil can be identified:

▫ **Moral** evil, which involves the responsibility of human actions that cause suffering or harm; for example, murder, stealing, lying.
▫ **Natural** evil, in which events related to nature, for example natural disasters and disease, cause suffering over which human beings have little or no control.

The problem of **suffering** has a slightly different emphasis, and this is a very important distinction. It focuses on the **experience** brought about by evil and raises different questions because of the experience. It deals with the problem on a more personal level. Questions such as 'Why me? Why now? Why this particular form? Why this intensity? Why this length?' are raised.

The logical problem of evil: classical version

The traditional 'logical' problem of evil and suffering arises when we consider the **co-existence** of **evil** and suffering in this world with the belief in a God who is all-powerful (**omnipotent**) and all-loving (**omnibenevolent**). Omnipotence also includes the concept of omniscience, since a God who can do anything but does not always know the best way to do it has to be less than all-powerful.

The problem has three aspects:

▫ Firstly, why is there evil in the world if there exists an omnipotent and omnibenevolent God who, by very definition, would **desire** and have the **power** to eliminate evil and suffering? Since evil and suffering do exist there is a logical inconsistency.
▫ The existence of evil and suffering can be explained if God wants to abolish evil but **cannot** (meaning that God is actually impotent not omnipotent).
▫ The existence of evil and suffering can be explained if God has the power to abolish evil but **will not** (meaning that God is actually wicked not all-loving).

In other words, if we accept that God is both all-powerful and good, then the assumption is that a good God would eliminate evil as far as he is able. Why does the God who has the power to eliminate all evil, not do so? God has the means (power) and the motivation (love, goodness) to eliminate evil but chooses not to.

If there is no God, then there is no problem and so essentially this is a **theistic problem**.

J. L. Mackie's modern development

Mackie developed the problem of evil by responding to theodicies that had been put forward to explain the existence of suffering and evil. He maintained that the triad of (1) evil and suffering (2) an omnipotent God and (3) an omnibenevolent God was inconsistent and could never be reconciled.

- ▣ The only solution would be to reject one aspect. Theodicies cannot do this, but Mackie pointed out that their 'success' depended upon re-interpreting the idea of omnipotence.
- ▣ In other words, the **theodicies misleadingly** kept the term '**omnipotence**' but actually weaken the meaning of the term so much so that it was not actually omnipotence.
- ▣ Mackie argues that the theodicies do not give a solution to the problem of evil since they have **changed the premise** (i.e. that God is omnipotent).
- ▣ Mackie proposed that the only way to consider omnipotence was in its full meaning.
- ▣ He pointed out what he called the '**Paradox of Omnipotence**' which is illustrated by a key question: 'Can an omnipotent being make things which he cannot subsequently control' or, '**make rules which bind** himself?'
- ▣ Mackie pointed out that to answer either **yes or no** would not be consistent with the concept of omnipotence:

1 If we answer 'yes, **God cannot remain omnipotent** once God has made them because there would be things which God cannot do.

2 If we answer 'no', we immediately affirm God is not omnipotent.

⁶TRIGGER QUOTES⁹

Either God cannot abolish evil, or he will not; if he cannot then he is not all-powerful; if he will not then he is not all-good. **(Augustine)**

Either God wants to abolish evil, and cannot; or he can, but does not want to. If he wants to, but cannot, he is impotent. If he can, but does not want to, he is wicked. If God can abolish evil, and God really wants to do it, why is there evil in the world? **(Epicurus)**

TIP

There are many named scholars in this section. Make sure that you are correct in attributing an idea to the relevant scholar.

⁶TRIGGER QUOTE⁹

Quite apart from the problem of evil, the Paradox of Omnipotence has shown that God's omnipotence must in any case be restricted in one way or another. **(J. L. Mackie)**

William Rowe and Gregory S. Paul

Specification Link

William Rowe (intense human and animal suffering) and Gregory S. Paul (premature deaths).

William Rowe is known for what is called the evidential problem of evil. His focus is on the extent of 'intense' suffering. In 1979 he published a critical paper entitled, 'The Problem of Evil and Some Varieties of Atheism' (American Philosophical Quarterly).

TRIGGER QUOTES

Even if you think it is reasonable to believe it in the case of the fawn, is it reasonable to believe it about every instance of seemingly pointless human and non-human animal suffering? **(W. Rowe)**

Intense human or animal suffering is in itself bad, an evil, even though it may sometimes be justified by virtue of being a part of, or leading to, some good which is unobtainable without it. **(W. Rowe)**

William Rowe: Evidential problem of evil

Rowe accepts the logical consistency of theistic proofs for God presented by the theodicies. He does not attack these. However, he presents his own thesis as follows:

1 There exist instances of **intense suffering** which an omnipotent, omniscient and wholly good being could prevent whilst not losing a greater good or allowing an evil equally bad or worse.

2 Such a being, by definition, would **prevent** any instances of intense suffering possible unless it would lose a greater good or allow an evil equally bad or worse.

3 There does not exist an omnipotent, omniscient, wholly good being.

◾ Rowe acknowledges that intense suffering of both humans and animals sometimes can be **justified as necessary** since, in and of itself, intense suffering should not be confused with a resulting greater good.

◾ For Rowe, these are basic moral principles shared by both theists and non-theists.

◾ However, the key to Rowe's argument is that there is evidence of instances where intense suffering **cannot be justified** or morally necessary.

◾ He uses the example of an isolated **forest fire** in which a **fawn** is trapped, horribly burned, and lies in terrible agony for several days before death relieves its suffering.

◾ The example of the fawn is an example of **unnecessary intense suffering**.

◾ The same principle could be applied to a human being.

◾ Although we cannot prove this intense suffering is unnecessary (as there may be some greater good that we are unaware of), Rowe makes a distinction between knowing what is true and having **rational grounds** for believing something to be true.

◾ Rowe argues that it 'seems quite unlikely that all the instances of intense suffering occurring daily in our world are intimately related to the occurrence of greater goods or the prevention of evils'.

◾ Therefore, Rowe concludes that there is a valid logical argument for atheism based upon the two premises:
(1) Instances of intense suffering do occur that an omnipotent, omniscient and wholly good being could prevent.
(2) As such instances are unnecessary but do occur then this is incompatible with an omnipotent, omniscient and wholly good being.

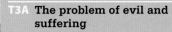

Gregory S. Paul: Statistical problem of evil

Gregory S. Paul contends that traditional theodicies and theistic arguments focus on '**nonquantitative arguments**', that is, they tend to be abstract and not base their arguments on empirical evidence such as **statistical data**.

Paul approaches the problem of suffering by focusing on evidence that demonstrates both the **extent** and **indiscriminate** nature of human suffering through **natural evil**. His basic thesis is:

Gregory S. Paul is a freelance academic scientist whose main area of interest is palaeontology, specialising in dinosaurs, but he has achieved international acclaim through his socio-theological articles on human suffering.

- ▣ Throughout history the statistical evidence for youth suffering and premature death is enormous.
- ▣ The figures are so high in relation to other suffering that they appear to be **maximised** beyond expectations – 'The **Holocaust of the Children**'.
- ▣ In light of such overwhelming evidence, the classic Christian **theodicies fail**, when confronted with the evidence of the extent of suffering and its 'arbitrarily discriminatory' occurrence.
- ▣ The main issue here for Paul is that there is a complete **denial of free will** to newborns and premature beings in particular.
- ▣ This cannot be reconciled with the existence of the God of classical theism.

Paul focuses on **demographic statistics** that detail the full extent and causes of suffering and early death of immature humans through natural evil. Paul's statistics cover pregnancy failures, infant and juvenile mortalities and third world childhood **deaths throughout history**, which, when added together, 'the estimated total prematurity loss of conceived humans is in the area of **350 billion**'.

Paul also considers disease, famine and malnutrition, together with earthquakes and floods for humanity in general. The statistics overall are devastating, but Paul argues that it is in the area of 'youth suffering and death' where it has had its greatest impact.

When Paul accounts for the proportion of such deaths that were due to natural evil, he concludes: 'all but a modest fraction of a few hundred billion humans have died before attaining maturity due to naturally evil causes not due to human moral evil'.

⟨**TRIGGER** QUOTES⟩

The Holocaust of the Children is so large in scale and depth that it poses such insurmountable problems for the classic Christian free will and best of all worlds hypotheses that they are falsified. **(G. S. Paul)**

It is said that God is in the details, and that the nature of creation reveals the nature of the creator. This is a valid point, but the implications are not necessarily what Christians wish for them to be. **(G. S. Paul)**

AO2

What is ... Evaluation and critical analysis ?

The AO2 skills of evaluation and critical analysis mean engaging with the controversies surrounding a subject. This is more than merely describing or listing the points made about a controversy. To achieve this, one weighs up strengths and weaknesses of various sides and takes a position. On the right are three controversies for each issue – you can engage in these by extending their arguments (adding examples, quotes or other details), weighing up their strengths and weaknesses, and coming to a conclusion.

⁶TRIGGER QUOTES⁹

... while remaining an evil in itself, the intense human or animal suffering is, nevertheless, an evil which someone might be morally justified in permitting.
(W. Rowe)

If a creator exists, then it has chosen to fashion a habitat that has maximised the level of suffering and deaths among young humans.
(G. S. Paul)

A quote can strengthen an argument you are making – but always be sure to include a sentence as to why the quote is important/relevant.

TIP

Issue:

The extent to which the classical form of the problem of evil is a problem

Three evaluative controversies!

▪ **Controversy 1:** *Is there a problem?*
The theodicies may be strained and uncomfortable, even for some believers, but a glimpse of hope in **reconciling** the traditional characteristics of God with the existence of evil is enough to solve the problem. However, for an **atheist** there may still be a problem. For example, it may well be that they have considered the problem and are **unconvinced** by the explanations on offer, such as that of Mackie. The extent of the problem, therefore, is directly related to how well a theodicy presents itself.

▪ **Controversy 2:** *Does the classical form focus enough on the real problem?*
Gregory Paul and William Rowe have demonstrated that the logical problem of evil is in fact a very **real problem** and not just a logical one. For Rowe, the evidential problem is the real issue in that actual instances of **unnecessary**, **intense suffering** can never be reconciled with an omnipotent and omnibenevolent God. For Paul, the overwhelming evidence that cannot be justified or explained away is the sheer **magnitude** of needless suffering and the denial of free will to premature and newborns. For Paul, on paper a theodicy may seem reasonable, but in reality, it does **not add up**.

▪ **Controversy 3:** *Do theodicies provide a rational answer?*
Rowe at least accepts that the **logic of theodicies** are viable and he can understand why believers may defend God; however, in the face of real instances of unnecessary, intense suffering he advocates a '**friendly atheism**' that acknowledges the need for some people to have such a theodicy in place whilst others may draw a reluctant and negative conclusion as to the existence of God based on the evidential problem. Alternatively, **Mackie** definitely rejects the logic of theodicies and has demonstrated the logical inconsistencies that they present. In light of this, however, one could consider the arguments presented by Process theologians that respond to Mackie's objections by denying God's absolute omnipotence in favour of a 'fellow sufferer who understands'. In such cases whilst the fact that evil still exists is an emotional and physical problem it is no longer a logical one.

Sp⊙tlight: **Evaluative judgements**

This section contains a special insight that you can use to form a judgement.

It is clear that the problem of evil and suffering is first and foremost a logical one. However, on closer analysis and dialogue, the problem itself may not be as unsolvable as some may assume. There are undeniably some issues and questions that are raised but is the answer as negative as the problem posed seems to suggest?

Issue:

The degree to which modern problem of evil arguments are effective in proving God's nonexistence

◼ Controversy 1: *Is Rowe's argument effective?*

It could be argued that William Rowe's argument transforms the logical problem into a practical one by appealing to **empirical evidence** and then testing the logical implication of what this means for God's will (omnibenevolent?) and power (omnipotent). In this sense it could be seen to be very effective. Rowe assumes an **interventionist God** and does not account for the thinking of Irenaean philosophers such as John Hick and his ideas about soul-making with further opportunities to develop in the afterlife and where all issues are reconciled. Rowe admits there may be a **bigger picture**; he rejects this as unlikely purely based on experience. Is this rejection valid?

◼ Controversy 2: *Is Paul's argument effective?*

The **statistical data** is so devastating that Paul appears very gloomy, depressing and, on the face of it, damning. His approach is one of appealing to the collective analysis of existence from a more **holistic perspective**. However, some would argue that the traditional response of deferment to the absolute and almighty nature of God is a valid response. In the Bible, **Job**, when all answers eluded him, came to accept the sovereignty of God when God declared: 'Where were you when I laid the earth's foundation? Tell me, if you understand.'

◼ Controversy 3: *Is Mackie's argument effective?*

Mackie's argument about the theodicies offered to answer the problem of evil and suffering was that each one had to re-define and clarify what the word **omnipotence** meant. That is, 'God is omnipotent but …' For Mackie this was a failure for the traditional understanding of God because they change the premise of the argument, i.e. the meaning of omnipotence and thus undermine its validity. It could be argued that Mackie fails to distinguish between having something and using it. To say God is omnipotent does not mean God can only do omnipotent things; God must be allowed to exercise the **full range of possible actions**. Similar to the idea behind Hick's epistemic distance, the **calculated step backwards** is not that God 'gives up' control or 'allows' freedom but that God exercises omnipotence within the full range of possibilities that omnipotence allows.

Is the problem of evil simply a logical one?

Quick Revision

Select two responses to the problem of evil that, in your opinion, are effective. Think about the reasons why you like them. Do the same for one response that you think is weak.

Sp⦿tlight: Evaluative judgements

This section contains a special insight that you can use to form a judgement.

Modern developments of the arguments surrounding the problem of evil and suffering, especially in the case of Rowe and Paul, tend to have shifted focus from abstract to the 'real world' using experiences and data to put forward their arguments.

AO1 Trigger revision activity

 A ZIP

Types of evil and the classical logical problem of evil

moral	co-existence	desire	will not
natural	evil	power	theistic problem
suffering	omnipotent	cannot	
experience	omnibenevolent		

1 Here is your zip file of portable Triggers.

2 Practise 'downloading' your zip file of Triggers from memory. See how many you can recall on first attempt.

3 When you are confident enough, order the Triggers into a list as you may do in an examination situation.

5 Now read through your descriptions and think about ways in which you could develop these using your Trigger quotes.

4 Attempt to write one clear sentence to define each Trigger.

 B ZIP

Modern development: Mackie, Paul and Rowe

changed the premise	justified as necessary	demographic statistics
omnipotence	prevent	natural evil
God cannot remain omnipotent	fawn	350 billion
yes or no	cannot be justified	deaths throughout history
'Paradox of Omnipotence'	forest fire	maximised
theodicies misleadingly	unnecessary intense suffering	indiscriminate
'make rules which bind		denial of free will
rational grounds		Holocaust of the Children

1 Fix the zip file! There are six Triggers missing from this zip file – find them and add them in.

2 There's another problem: the Triggers are out of order! Put them in the same order as they appear in the AO1 section above.

3 Practise 'downloading' your zip file of Triggers from memory. See how many you can recall on first attempt.

6 Now read through your definitions and think about ways in which you could develop these using your Trigger quotes.

5 Attempt to write one clear sentence to define each Trigger.

4 When you are confident enough, order the Triggers into a list as you may do in an examination situation.

AO2 Trigger revision activity

A
ZIP

The problem with the classical problem of evil

problem?	real problem	rational answer
reconciling	unnecessary, intense suffering	logic of theodicies
atheist	not add up	'friendly atheism'
unconvinced	Magnitude	Mackie

1 Here is your zip file of portable Triggers.

2 Practise 'downloading' your zip file of Triggers from memory. See how many you can recall on first attempt.

3 When you are confident enough, order the Triggers into a list as you may do in an examination situation.

5 Now read through all your sentences and think about ways in which you could develop these using your Trigger quotes, further examples, and noting strengths and weaknesses.

4 'Double-click' each Trigger in your memory – what can you say about an evaluative point of view in a clear sentence? Write this down. Do this for each Trigger in turn.

REVISION TIP

Using Trigger quotes
When you choose the Trigger quotes that you wish to use make sure that you explain how they are relevant.

B
ZIP

Are modern problem of evil arguments effective?

Paul's argument	Mackie's argument	holistic perspective
interventionist God	omnipotence	theologians
bigger picture	statistical data	empirical evidence

1 Fix the zip file! There are three Triggers missing from this zip file – find them and add them in.

2 There's another problem: the Triggers are out of order! Put them in the same order as they appear in the AO2 section above.

3 Practise 'downloading' your zip file of Triggers from memory. See how many you can recall on first attempt.

6 Now read through all your sentences and think about ways in which you could develop these using your Trigger quotes, further examples, and noting strengths and weaknesses.

5 Attempt to write one clear sentence to define each Trigger.

4 When you are confident enough, order the Triggers into a list as you may do in an examination situation.

Specification Link

Evil as a consequence of sin: evil as a privation; the fall of human beings and creation; the Cross overcomes evil, soul-deciding.

AO1

What is ...
Knowledge and
understanding ?

This is the skill that involves *selecting* the relevant and appropriate information, *organising* it and then *presenting* it through a *personal explanation* that may involve the use of supporting *evidence* and *examples*.

A theodicy can be more about the integrity of God's character being on trial rather than the debate about existence.

Spot the Triggers!
The words in blue are Triggers – key words and phrases that can help you remember knowledge and understanding in this area.

TIP

Theme 3B: Religious responses to the problem of evil

Augustinian type theodicy

- The actual existence of evil and suffering poses a major problem for theology. If God is totally good, and, in Augustine's view, the created order was perfect, then how did evil arise? What are its **origins**? If God created everything, then does this include evil?
- Another issue directly arises from this first set of questions, namely, what **purpose** do evil and suffering serve?
- It is these questions that have caused theologians to respond in order to make sense of both the logical and evidential problem of evil in both its moral and natural forms.
- Although this had been discussed by many theologians way back before Augustine, the term '**theodicy**' – which is used to describe a defence of a just God – was first used by the German philosopher Leibniz.
- Theodicy translates literally as '**justifying God**' but this can be misleading as it is not justifying God's existence but rather trying to demonstrate that the concept of an omnipotent, omnibenevolent God is compatible with evil and suffering. The word 'dike' (Greek) has been translated as 'custom', 'justice', 'right' and even 'court case'.
- In some ways a theodicy is like **God on trial**, investigating where the responsibility for evil and suffering lies.

The Specification refers to 'Augustinian type theodicy' and not 'Augustine's theodicy' for two reasons:

- Augustine did not have a fully worked-out theodicy. He approached the issue of the problem of evil from a variety of perspectives or themes in a variety of different writings.
- These general **themes** have been the basis of a number of writings by different theologians throughout the centuries which reflect the traditional Christian approach.

The main themes of an Augustinian type theodicy are:

- God's creation was **perfect**, including human beings.
- Human beings have free will but used their free will to turn away from God (**the Fall**).
- Human beings inherit Adam's **original sin**.
- The created order was affected by the Fall ('cursed is the ground because of you' Genesis 3:17).
- Natural evils are the outworking of this curse (but also due to the influence of fallen angels – Augustine seems to have accepted a 'warfare theodicy' at times).
- Evil is not a substance but a **privation of good**.

- Human **perception of evil** is due to our inability to see holistically as God does.
- God has made possible repentance and **salvation** through Christ.

The Augustinian type theodicy is sometimes referred to as '**soul-deciding**', although there is debate about what precisely this refers to.

The Fall of human beings and creation theme

- God created human beings with **free will**, which necessarily includes the concept of **moral responsibility**. Adam and Eve were the first humans to exercise their free will in God's creation (Genesis 3) but were **tempted** by the serpent (Satan) to disobey God.
- Eve was the first to disobey by eating fruit from the forbidden tree of the knowledge of good and evil; she then persuaded Adam to do the same. God **punished** Eve first, then Adam.
- Through sin and punishment, the created order was directly affected, evil entered the created order, **death** was introduced ('dust you are and to dust you will return') and Adam and Eve were banished from the garden that contained the tree of the knowledge of good and evil.
- This episode is known as the Fall (from Grace) and Augustine argued that human beings were all '**seminally present**' in Adam's sin; since we all share his guilt and sin, we all deserve to face the same punishment.

Evil as a consequence of sin and a privation of good theme

- Augustine was extremely keen to answer the question of whether or not, as ultimate being, God created evil. This was a major problem.
- Since God is good, then **evil cannot arise from God**.
- As a result of the Fall, natural order was affected.
- Augustine went further to argue that evil is **not a substance**, something that exists, but is simply a consequence of 'fallenness'.
- He called this a '**privation of good**', that is, a lack of good as opposed to the presence of evil. Thus 'evil' has no real substance and God cannot be thought of as having created it.
- A privation is the absence or lack of something that ought to be there. It is the **malfunctioning** of something that in itself is good. For instance, sickness is a real physical lack of good health.
- Evil cannot exist in its own right. Evil happens when something renounces its proper role in the divine scheme and ceases to be what it is meant to be. Hence moral evil is the privation of right order in the human will.
- Our rebellion against God has affected all of creation and distorted it, so that our environment is not as God intended it (Romans 8:22).
- In addition, Augustine saw natural evil caused by **fallen angels** who by their free decisions wreak havoc.

❝TRIGGER QUOTES❞

For evil has no positive nature; but the loss of good has received the name 'evil'. **(Augustine)**

For evil is the absence of the good, which is natural and due to a thing. **(Augustine)**

TIP

Remember, we do not need to discuss the life of Augustine when we answer questions on Augustinian type theodicies.

Quick Revision

Make a list of all the Triggers, cut them out and then mix them up. See if you can make some order from them without looking at the book.

The Cross overcomes evil: soul-deciding theme

- The Augustine theodicy sees evil as spoiling the perfect world that God created.
- The death of **Jesus** is seen as the **ultimate solution** to evil and through the effects of that event, evil can be overcome.
- One of Augustine's strongest themes is that God can **bring good from evil** and so the idea of Christ overcoming the effects of the Fall transforms it into a '**happy mistake**' (felix culpa).
- Augustine's theodicy is often referred to as **soul-deciding** due to the fact the notion of free will is integral to the events surrounding the Fall of humanity since the Fall was a decision of disobedience by a free human will but yet also able to **accept redemption** through Christ.
- With that freedom comes the possibility of **choosing evil**; free will, enacted wrongly, spoils God's perfect creation.
- Augustine argues that God **foresaw** the Fall 'from the foundation of the world' and planned redemption through Christ.
- This not only demonstrates that God is merciful but also that it underlines God's just nature.

Challenges to Augustinian type theodicies

Theological and philosophical challenges: the validity of accounts in Genesis, Chapters 2 and 3

- For those who accept the authority of scripture, Augustine's argument appears valid as it tends towards a **literal** reading interspersed with corresponding allegorical understanding. However, the centrality of Genesis 1–3 to the theodicy weakens the argument, as the literal interpretation of Genesis seems contrary to **modern thinking**.
- Accordingly, as soon as any other view of scripture is taken, Augustine's theodicy becomes problematic. For example, a non-literary reading directly challenges the theodicy and makes it suspect.
- **John Hick** in his *Evil and the God of Love* (1966) considers many of these problems. Hick rejects the idea of evil being a privation and so cannot reconcile an omnipotent God with evil and suffering unless an explanation is accepted other than that offered by Augustine.

Theological and philosophical challenges: moral contradictions of omnibenevolent God and existence of Hell

- It is hard to clear God from responsibility for evil since he chose to create a being whom he **foresaw** would do evil.
- The view that evil is not a substance and therefore not created by God, seems to free God from responsibility for evil. However, Augustine's view of evil as a **privation** is challenged. It is not sufficient to say that it is a lack, or absence, and many would argue that it is a real entity that needs to be explained.
- If everything depends on God for its existence, then God must be **causally involved** in free human actions. Do we have free will? Augustine faced this issue when he was confronted with the Pelagian controversy and developed his concept of predestination.

❛TRIGGER QUOTE❜

Intense human or animal suffering is in itself bad, an evil, even though it may sometimes be justified by virtue of being a part of, or leading to, some good which is unobtainable without it.
(W. Rowe)

- The concept of **Hell** being part of the created order suggests that not only did God know that angels and human beings would fall, but he had also prepared a place of punishment for them. This is not consistent with the concept of an all-loving God.
- Augustine establishes that creation was **perfect**, but if this is the case then humans who are given free will would not sin, otherwise they were not **flawless** to start with! This means God must share the responsibility of their fall.
- Hick argues that Augustine's theodicy needs to be understood in the **historical context** of theological views at the time and therefore, as such, it has no relevance to the way in which we understand the world today.

Scientific challenges: the error of original sin

- One of the major criticisms of Augustine's theodicy is the idea of 'original sin' and that humans were '**seminally present**' in the loins of Adam and so morally take on the responsibility and consequences of his actions.
- Many scientists would argue the idea of descending from an original single male and female couple is **not scientifically possible**.
- If that is the case, then the whole idea of genetic culpability is demolished.
- 'Sin' and moral consequences cannot be **transferred** in this way.
- Dawkins speaks of '**memes**' and inherited tendencies to behave in a certain way and although this could be used in support of Augustinian type theodicies.
- The argument is weak because the problem then arises that this behavioural trait is not consistent, but is, according to the principles of evolution, subject to change.
- Accordingly, the idea of 'inheritance' from a very specific characteristic originating in a single pair of human beings is questionable.

Scientific challenges: the contradiction of perfect order becoming chaotic

- Augustine seems to account successfully for the occurrence of natural evil. However, **modern science** challenges the picture of a fall of humanity from perfection and the subsequent disruption of the created order.
- Scientific understanding suggests that there was an **evolutionary** development and not a sudden change; the process of natural selection, mutation and evolution from earlier life forms is well evidenced.
- **Geologists** see the world as chaotic and complex.
- Evolution has no inherent value judgement; there is **no intrinsic directionality** towards 'advancement' but simply each evolved species is a result of locating their niche within their environment.

Can the idea of Hell ever be reconciled with an omnibenevolent God?

6 *TRIGGER* QUOTES 9

I've always leant on original sin in a difficult moment because it transfers the blame from me to everyone. **(R. Scruton)**

Original sin itself comes straight from the Old Testament myth of Adam and Eve. Their sin – eating the fruit of a forbidden tree – seems mild enough to merit a mere reprimand. **(R. Dawkins)**

Nature therefore which has been corrupted, is called evil, for assuredly when incorrupt it is good; but even when corrupt, so far as it is nature it is good, so far as it is corrupted it is evil. **(Augustine)**

Quick Revision

Select what you think are the five most important Trigger challenges from philosophy, theology and science and explain why they are important to our understanding of the problem of evil.

AO2

What is ... Evaluation and critical analysis

The AO2 skills of evaluation and critical analysis mean engaging with the controversies surrounding a subject. This is more than merely describing or listing the points made about a controversy. To achieve this, one weighs up strengths and weaknesses of various sides and takes a position. On the right are three controversies for each issue – you can engage in these by extending their arguments (adding examples, quotes or other details), weighing up their strengths and weaknesses, and coming to a conclusion.

6 TRIGGER QUOTES 9

People said to be cruel or evil are simply at one extreme of the empathy spectrum.
(S. Baron-Cohen)

Any defence of Augustine's position has to begin by pointing out that his account of evil is metaphysical rather than empirical.
(C. Carlisle)

When presenting views of others, make sure that they are relevant to the focus of the question. An argument presented by yourself that is directly relevant to the focus of the question is more creditworthy than referring to a scholar whose views are not addressing the issues.

Issue:

Whether Augustinian type theodicies are relevant in the 21st century

Three evaluative controversies!

- **Controversy 1:** *Is the idea of a created order becoming instantly disordered coherent?*
  The problem with Augustinian type theodicies is that there are themes that cannot really be justified today, especially the idea of a created order that was **perfect** and then became imperfect. **Geological** and **biological** evidence seems to suggest that this is not possible. However, a theologian may argue that this is because firstly there is now chaos and the biblical accounts focus more on **order prior to chaos**, and secondly, a consequence of the Fall is that we cannot understand or see the full picture due to our ignorance compared to God's omniscience.

- **Controversy 2:** *Does the theodicy reflect teachings of the Church today?*
  In general, a significant proportion of the worldwide **Church today accepts** the teachings of Augustine. Nevertheless, there are some Christians who have challenged and questioned the relevance of Augustinian type theodicies. **John Hick**, for example, rejects the idea that human beings were created as perfect and presents an alternative line of reasoning that free will entails growth and development, learning from mistakes. For Hick, evil and suffering cannot be seen as privation of good but are **real entities** that people have to deal with as part of this journey.

- **Controversy 3:** *Is evil as a privation acceptable today?*
  Clare Carlisle has described evil as 'a deep, impenetrable darkness that resists the light of reason' by which we mean that an evil murderer does not possess evil as a substance, but rather, that we mean there is an **'an absence of motive'**. Although some would say that the survival mechanisms inherent in evolutionary theory are **morally neutral** and that what we call evil is simply part of the world in which we live, Carlisle points out that Augustine's 'privation' is similar to the proposal by psychopathologist Simon Baron-Cohen that evil is simply **'empathy erosion'**, something that is socially lacking or 'a disruption of normal functioning'.

Spotlight: **Evaluative judgements**

This section contains a special insight that you can use to form a judgement.

Another challenge to the effects of the Fall on the created order is the issue of animal suffering. Whilst Augustine can readily explain animal suffering in terms of human moral evil and natural evil (disease, etc.) the theodicy does not reflect attitudes today towards animals. Why did other beings suffer because of a human mistake? It appears they are innocent victims. Why are animals not offered the same opportunity of redemption as are humans?

Issue:

The extent to which Augustine's theodicy succeeds as a defence of the God of classical theism

◻ **Controversy 1:** *Does it have to be a complete package?*

As a complete package it would appear that Augustine's theodicy is not totally successful in defending the God of classical theism because there are essential issues with the idea of the Fall, such as reconciling the view of **hereditary sin** with a good and **merciful deity** that could not punish an innocent new born or hold them accountable for another individual's error. However, its success has been supported by the fact it has remained a **very popular** response within the Church itself and as a complete package it does provide an explanation.

◻ **Controversy 2:** *Are free will and complete omnipotence logically consistent?*

Augustine is absolute in his belief about free will and **human accountability**. However, this caused problems for him when he came to guard the Church against **Pelagian** heresies where he had to stress the absolute and unconditional **omnipotence** of God. However, it could be argued that Adam's 'accountability' can be reconciled with unconditional omnipotence by distinguishing the Original Sin of Adam from our sins – the former comes out of freedom and the latter does not.

◻ **Controversy 3:** *What about the problem of original sin?*

The idea of original sins remains a major weakness in Augustine's defence of the God of classical theism. One could ask why would an **all-loving God** hold an individual responsible for another's sin? If the acceptance of redemption and salvation is an individual process, then why does **Adam's accountability** for sin not hold the same individual value? Theologically, as Pelagius also pointed out, the theory does have problems without even considering the issue of free will in its purest sense. However, scientifically this also has major issues. How can we accept the idea of hereditary sinfulness today when there is **no empirical evidence** that would support this? It would appear, then, that Augustine's idea of original sin impacts upon how successful he is at defending the God of classical theism.

> **❝TRIGGER QUOTE❞**
>
> I defend cognitive dualism: that the world can be understood completely in another way which also has its truths which are not translatable into the truths of science.
>
> **(R. Scruton)**

The Roman Catholic Church supports Augustinian type theodicies.

Spotlight: Evaluative judgements

This section contains a special insight that you can use to form a judgement.

The problem of evil and suffering has long remained the most popular response given by people to justify a rejection of belief in a God who is supposed to be omnipotent and omnibenevolent. Your evaluation of this issue should recognise that there are many aspects of, and implications for, the views expressed in the debate.

Quick Revision

Try to think of which themes of an Augustinian type theodicy are strong and those themes which you feel are problematic. Try to express your own reasons for this and not just the views of others.

AO1 Trigger revision activity

A

Augustinian type theodicies / themes

1 There are no Triggers in this zip file! Find and add in the relevant Triggers.

2 Now put the Triggers in the same order as they appear in the AO1 section above.

3 Practise 'downloading' your zip file of Triggers from memory. See how many you can recall on first attempt.

6 Now read through your definitions and think about ways in which you could develop these using your Trigger quotes.

5 Attempt to write one clear sentence to define each Trigger.

4 When you are confident enough, order the Triggers into a list as you may do in an examination situation.

B

Challenges to the theodicies: scientific and philosophical

literal	perfect	'memes'
modern thinking	flawless	modern science
John Hick	historical context	evolutionary
privation	seminally present'	geologists
foresaw	not scientifically possible	no intrinsic directionality
causally involved	sin	
Hell	transferred	

1 Here is your zip file of portable Triggers.

2 Practise 'downloading' your zip file of Triggers from memory. See how many you can recall on first attempt.

3 When you are confident enough, order the Triggers into a list as you may do in an examination situation.

5 Now read through your descriptions and think about ways in which you could develop these using your Trigger quotes.

4 Attempt to write one clear sentence to define each Trigger.

AO2 Trigger revision activity

A **ZIP**

Are Augustinian type theodicies still relevant today?

1 There are no Triggers in this zip file! Find and add in the relevant Triggers. →

2 Now put the Triggers in the same order as they appear in the AO2 section above. →

3 Practise 'downloading' your zip file of Triggers from memory. See how many you can recall on first attempt.

6 Now read through all your sentences and think about ways in which you could develop these using your Trigger quotes, further examples, and noting strengths and weaknesses. ←

5 Attempt to write one clear sentence to define each Trigger. ←

4 When you are confident enough, order the Triggers into a list as you may do in an examination situation.

B **ZIP**

The effectiveness of Augustinian type theodicies

complete package	logically consistent	all-loving God
hereditary sin	human accountability	Adam's accountability
merciful deity	omnipotence	no empirical evidence
very popular	original sin	Pelagian

1 Here is your zip file of portable Triggers. →

2 Practise 'downloading' your zip file of Triggers from memory. See how many you can recall on first attempt.

5 Now read through all your sentences and think about ways in which you could develop these using your Trigger quotes, further examples, and noting strengths and weaknesses. ←

4 'Double-click' each Trigger in your memory – what can you say about an evaluative point of view in a clear sentence? Write this down. Do this for each Trigger in turn. ←

REVISION TIP

Using Trigger quotes
When you choose the Trigger quotes that you wish to use make sure that you explain how they are relevant.

3 When you are confident enough, order the Triggers into a list as you may do in an examination situation.

Specification Link

Religious responses to the problem of evil (ii): Irenaean type theodicy: Vale of soul-making: human beings created imperfect; epistemic distance; second-order goods; eschatological justification.

AO1

**What is ...
Knowledge and
understanding?**

This is the skill that involves *selecting* the relevant and appropriate information, *organising* it and then *presenting* it through a *personal explanation* that may involve the use of supporting *evidence* and *examples*.

John Hick: 1922–2012. Hick was one of the most influential religious philosophers of the twentieth and early twenty-first centuries.

❝ TRIGGER QUOTE ❞

But the man was a little one, and his discretion still undeveloped, wherefore also he was easily misled by the deceiver.

(Irenaeus)

Theme 3C: Religious responses to the problem of evil

Irenaean type theodicies

- Irenaeus, like Augustine, did not have a systematic theodicy but his ideas have been used by theologians to present theodicies that develop his observations.
- In terms of responsibility for the **existence of evil** and suffering, Irenaeus begins with the understanding that **God is responsible** and that this was deliberate with **good reason**.
- This is because God wanted human beings to **develop** the qualities that would make them **spiritually perfect**.
- Irenaeus uses the first part of Genesis 1:26, which reads: 'Then God said, "Let us make humankind in our **image**, according to our **likeness**"'.
- Although Irenaeus did not make such a sharp distinction between the 'image' and the 'likeness' of God that later medieval theologians and John Hick did, the position of Irenaeus was clear that human beings were created with only **partial maturity**, made with the **potential** to develop and grow into the image and likeness of God.
- According to Irenaeus, Adam and Eve were expelled from the Garden of Eden not because they were perfect and then sinned, but because they were immature.
- Medieval theologians, and recently the philosopher John Hick, introduced a **distinction** between 'image' (possessing the potential qualities of God's spiritual perfection) and 'likeness' (actualising those qualities) to help support Irenaeus' ideas.
- **John Hick** also rejected a literal reading of the Fall from a 'perfect state' and focused on the idea of eschatological perfection through Christ. Some would describe his **evolutionary** ideas as more pertinent to the modern world.
- For Hick, the Fall was an inevitable part of this growing up and maturing and that evil and suffering are essential for this development to occur.
- The created order then becomes the arena of opportunity for this development, or, as Hick stated, 'a **vale of soul-making**'.
- An essential part of this theodicy is that this process is worthwhile because of the **eventual outcome** of salvation.
- **Free will** and the ability to choose to do good was essential for this growth and development.
- Hick argues that in order to be totally free, there must be an '**epistemic distance**' between God and humanity.
- This means that human beings are unaware of the knowledge of God and have to make spiritual and moral decisions themselves and freely choose to accept God through faith.

- The epistemic distance is seen as **superior** to the scenario of a God who (i) creates perfect creatures with ready made goodness and (ii) watches his creation so that all decisions are made in light of the watchful eye of God. Epistemic distance eliminates these interpretations.
- Hick argued that God's **mercy** allows all those who do not accept God, or those who have no opportunity to mature, to continue this process in the afterlife.
- This 'eschatological justification' for the existence of evil and suffering demonstrates that God is both merciful and just.

Challenges to Irenaean type theodicies

The concept of universal salvation is unjust

- The idea of everyone eventually achieving the goal of salvation makes **moral behaviour** in the present life **redundant** – what is the point if I will be saved anyway?
- If everyone is to achieve salvation then do I really have the free will to refuse it? At the very least **free will is limited**.

Evil and suffering should not be used as a tool by an omnibenevolent God

- Suffering should never be an instrument of a loving God. Hurting someone is more akin to **abuse** than it is to love.
- The idea of using evil and suffering makes God into a **tyrant** who is exercising power or control in a cruel, unreasonable, and arbitrary way.
- Surely there are **better ways** to achieve spiritual and moral development?
- Why would it not be acceptable to have **more help** and guidance so that we can mature?
- Why does the process **take so long** and can we really expect people to accept the belief that it will be better in the afterlife without any certainty?
- Finally, as a Christian theodicy, it appears to challenge the **role of Jesus** as saviour and atoning (making amends) for all sins.

Immensity of suffering and unequal distribution of evil and suffering

- To suggest that an all-loving God would use evil and suffering as a tool for learning may sound reasonable in theory, but the reality of the **amount of misery** caused is too **extreme** and **totally unnecessary**.
- This is also **not worth the prize** of spiritual perfection. How can the evil and suffering associated with Auschwitz during the Holocaust or random acts of terror killing innocents be adequate justification for the end – salvation?
- Not only the intensity of the suffering is challenged but also the **arbitrary** nature of how this is distributed amongst humanity and throughout history.
- The reality of the theodicy is that it is **unrealistic** when presented with empirical evidence and statistics.
- Some would therefore describe this as a '**soul-breaking**' rather than a 'soul-making' theodicy.

TRIGGER QUOTE

it is an ethically reasonable judgement.... that human goodness slowly built up through personal histories of moral effort has a value in the eyes of the Creator. **(J. Hick)**

Specification Link

Challenges to Irenaean type theodicies: concept of universal salvation unjust; evil and suffering should not be used as a tool by an omnibenevolent God; immensity of suffering and unequal distribution of evil and suffering.

Quick Revision

Try to identify the basic theodicy of Irenaeus and the ideas added by John Hick to develop this by creating a two-coloured list of the essential points above.

Is the horrendous evil and unimaginable suffering of the Holocaust justified by any theodicy?

TRIGGER QUOTE

The common cognomen of this world among the misguided and superstitious is 'a vale of tears' from which we are to be redeemed by a certain arbitrary interposition of God and taken to Heaven. **(J. Keats)**

TIP

One of the criticisms of soul-making is only a strong criticism if a person holds to a Christian view of the atonement. If they don't then it holds no value as a criticism.

AO2

What is ... Evaluation and critical analysis

The AO2 skills of evaluation and critical analysis mean engaging with the controversies surrounding a subject. This is more than merely describing or listing the points made about a controversy. To achieve this, one weighs up strengths and weaknesses of various sides and takes a position. On the right are three controversies for each issue – you can engage in these by extending their arguments (adding examples, quotes or other details), weighing up their strengths and weaknesses, and coming to a conclusion.

6 TRIGGER QUOTES 9

God made man a free [agent] from the beginning ... there is no coercion with God.   **(Irenaeus)**

And the harder we strive, so much is it the more valuable.   **(Irenaeus)**

TIP
One of the skills of critical analysis is to make comment on views presented. Make sure that you put forward your opinions based on the evidence presented, not just at the end of an answer but throughout it.

Issue:
Whether Irenaean type theodicies are credible in the 21st century

Three evaluative controversies!

▫ **Controversy 1:** *Is the idea of an evolutionary development valid?*
This theodicy, on the face of it, seems consistent with **modern thinking** about origins of life. Some may argue that this idea fits in with a modern 21st-century scientific understanding that life on earth develops qualities that help it survive more effectively within the natural environment, known as **natural selection**. However, the comparisons with the idea of evolution are **weak**. Evolution is based upon the harsh reality of the survival of the fittest – how could compassion be developed in this scenario? Equally evolution does not necessarily equate to development towards an end goal and is dictated by the surrounding environment and not a higher purpose. What goal did dinosaurs achieve?

▫ **Controversy 2:** *Are the modern arguments compelling?*
Rowe and Paul delivered devastating challenges to any theodicy with evidential and **statistical arguments**. The sheer volume and unjust distribution of evil and suffering appears to be **inconsistent** with the Irenaean theodicy when it is applied to the real world. Is the evidence from Rowe and Paul strong enough to defeat the Irenaean theodicy? Not necessarily so. There are actually people who have the **real experience** of intense, unnecessary suffering and yet still would accept the Irenaean theodicy through faith. The question is, would it be unfair to simply point out they are mistaken or is there something that even evidence cannot explain?

▫ **Controversy 3:** *Is there enough support for this today?*
21st-century thinking has the advantage of being able to access all **cumulative debate** about issues relating to the problem of evil and suffering that have been raised throughout history so far. These are then **tested against** a theodicy that is historically cited and cannot support itself, unless by the means of religious believers who simply replicate or expand the argument. There is support from the likes of **Alvin Plantinga** who develops the free will defence and the best of all possible worlds. There is support also, indirectly, from such as Maurice Wiles who argues that an interventionist God is not morally acceptable. Finally, the fierce challenges that **John Hick**'s ideas face, in terms of the evidential and statistical data, question the viability of support for an Irenaean type theodicy.

Sp☼tlight: Evaluative judgements
This section contains a special insight that you can use to form a judgement.

Theologians, such as John Hick and Alvin Plantinga, have demonstrated that the ideas of free will in order to mature or create the best possible environment to exercise freedom are still relevant ideas in the 21st century. However, the real issue is whether or not they are adequate explanations and justifications for the God of classical theism for the 21st-century mind.

Issue:

The extent to which Irenaeus's theodicy succeeds as a defence of the God of classical theism

- **Controversy 1: *Is it a successful defence of the God of classical theism to argue that evil is a tool for a greater good?***
  Irenaeus' defence for the existence of evil and suffering is that it is all a part of **God's plan** for humanity. In doing so, Irenaeus is acknowledging the 'third corner' of the inconsistent triad and attempting to explain this by stating that there is a higher **purpose for evil**, namely, to achieve spiritual and moral perfection. This, in theory, does successfully answer the problem posed by the inconsistent triad. The issue here is whether we can accept the **gravity and severity** of the means to an end and for many people this fails in the light of the omnipotence and, in particular, the omnibenevolence of God.

- **Controversy 2: *Is there any point to eschatological justification?***
  Irenaeus also argues that it is God's mercy that justifies the means of evil and suffering because the journey to **spiritual maturity** extends beyond this life. Furthermore, in the afterlife, there is not only the opportunity to overcome evil and suffering but the guarantee that it will be overcome for all individuals who will receive **salvation**. There appears to be an inconsistency that this brings. If a person can develop further into maturity in the afterlife then how would they do this if evil and **suffering is essential** for that development? Either evil and suffering must therefore exist in the afterlife, or, to be consistent one must argue that there are more rebirths in which an individual must endure which only prolong the process even more!

- **Controversy 3: *If God is omnipotent, then there must be an alternative way.***
  Part of omnipotence is omniscience and so the success of the Irenaean type theodicy rests upon the understanding that God knows that this is the **best possible way** to achieve the goal of spiritual maturity without compromising free will. However, Rowe challenges the logic that this is the best way as he argues that there are indeed **episodes of pointless suffering** that are unnecessary and that could be overturned without contradiction by an omnipotent God. Paul challenges this from the perspective of statistical information; the sheer volume of evil and suffering does add up and not make sense. Moreover, it appears also **arbitrary** and inconsistent in its distribution.

> **TRIGGER QUOTES**
>
> The argument is valid; therefore, if we have rational grounds for accepting its premises, to that extent we have rational grounds for accepting atheism. **(W. Rowe)**
>
> The Holocaust of the Children bars an enormous portion of humans from making a decision about their eternal fate while maximising the suffering of children. **(G. S. Paul)**

Can the end goal ever justify the means of evil and suffering?

Quick Revision

One of the skills of evaluation is to raise pertinent questions in response to views presented. As you go through your revision, make a list of questions you would like to ask based on the evidence presented, not just at the end of an answer but throughout it.

Sp⬤tlight: **Evaluative judgements**

This section contains a special insight that you can use to form a judgement.

Why did the natural environment have to be created through a long, slow, pain-filled evolutionary process? Why could an omnipotent God not do it in 'the twinkling of an eye'? These are two key questions that face the Irenaean type theodicy. How can we accept both the existence of an omnipotent, omnibenevolent God with the existence of suffering and evil?

AO1 Trigger revision activity

A

ZIP

Irenaean type theodicies

partial maturity	develop	eventual outcome
existence of evil	spiritually perfect	free will
mercy	image	superior
God is responsible	epistemic distance	eschatological justification
distinction	likeness	potential
good reason	vale of soul-making	

1 Fix the zip file! There are two Triggers missing from this zip file – find them and add them in. →

2 There's another problem: the Triggers are out of order! Put them in the same order as they appear in the AO1 section above. →

3 Practise 'downloading' your zip file of Triggers from memory. See how many you can recall on first attempt.

6 Now read through your definitions and think about ways in which you could develop these using your Trigger quotes. ←

5 Attempt to write one clear sentence to define each Trigger. ←

4 When you are confident enough, order the Triggers into a list as you may do in an examination situation.

B

ZIP

Challenges to Irenaean type theodicies

1 There are no Triggers in this zip file! Find and add in the relevant Triggers. →

2 Now put the Triggers in the same order as they appear in the AO1 section above. →

3 Practise 'downloading' your zip file of Triggers from memory. See how many you can recall on first attempt.

6 Now read through your definitions and think about ways in which you could develop these using your Trigger quotes. ←

5 Attempt to write one clear sentence to define each Trigger. ←

4 When you are confident enough, order the Triggers into a list as you may do in an examination situation.

AO2 Trigger revision activity

A   ZIP

Is the Irenaean theodicy credible in the 21st century?

John Hick	cumulative debate	statistical arguments
inconsistent	tested against	real experience
evolutionary development	weak	modern thinking

1 Fix the zip file! There are three Triggers missing from this zip file – find them and add them in.

2 There's another problem: the Triggers are out of order! Put them in the same order as they appear in the AO2 section above.

3 Practise 'downloading' your zip file of Triggers from memory. See how many you can recall on first attempt.

6 Now read through all your sentences and think about ways in which you could develop these using your Trigger quotes, further examples, and noting strengths and weaknesses.

5 Attempt to write one clear sentence to define each Trigger.

4 When you are confident enough, order the Triggers into a list as you may do in an examination situation.

B   ZIP

The success of the Irenaean theodicy

1 There are no Triggers in this zip file! Find and add in the relevant Triggers.

2 Now put the Triggers in the same order as they appear in the AO2 section above.

3 Practise 'downloading' your zip file of Triggers from memory. See how many you can recall on first attempt.

6 Now read through all your sentences and think about ways in which you could develop these using your Trigger quotes, further examples, and noting strengths and weaknesses.

5 Attempt to write one clear sentence to define each Trigger.

4 When you are confident enough, order the Triggers into a list as you may do in an examination situation.

Theme 4A: **The nature of religious experience**

Visions

AO1

What is ... Knowledge and understanding ?

This is the skill that involves *selecting* the relevant and appropriate information, *organising* it and then *presenting* it through a *personal explanation* that may involve the use of supporting *evidence* and *examples*.

Spot the Triggers!
The words in blue are Triggers – key words and phrases that can help you remember knowledge and understanding in this area.

TIP

❝ *TRIGGER* QUOTES ❞

I saw the Lord sitting on a throne.
(Isaiah 6:1)

... having been warned in a dream not to return to Herod, they [the wise men] left for their own country by another road.
(Matthew 2:12)

❝ *TRIGGER* QUOTES ❞

...a self hitherto divided, and consciously wrong, inferior and unhappy, becomes unified and consciously right, superior and happy...
(W. James)

In the Trinity term of 1929 I gave in, and admitted that God was God, and knelt and prayed.
(C. S. Lewis)

- A **vision** involves 'seeing something' **beyond normal** experience.
- **Features** of a vision include sensory aspects, dream/trance qualities, and intellectual content (i.e. there may be a 'message' that comes with the vision).
- In a vision with **sensory** aspects the recipient experiences a sight, sound, smell or feel that is extraordinary; this can include seeing a corporeal (physical) object. (for example, the bright lights that blinded Paul in Acts 9).
- Visions may also be thought to occur in a **dream** or in one's imagination. (for example, the wise men received a warning in a dream – Matthew 2).
- Many visions are accompanied by **intellectual content** – this can be a message of inspiration, insight or instruction (example: Peter being told that all foods are 'clean' – see Acts 10).
- Visions have been claimed to have been experienced by both **groups and individuals** (group: Angel of Mons; individual: Bernadette of Lourdes instructed by Mary to find a healing well).
- Examples of religious visions include **Guru Nanak**'s vision of God's court, Ezekiel's vision of God in the cloud, and some Muslims might see Muhammad's experience in the cave at Mount Hira as a vision.
- A vision can form a part of another type of religious experience such as prayer, conversion or mysticism (such as Paul's conversion involving a sensory vision).

Conversion

- 'Conversion' means, literally, **turning around**. In religion, it usually refers to a change in beliefs or orientation.
- Conversion can be a **collective or individual** experience.
- Collective conversion examples: the crowd who repented after Peter's sermon in Acts 2 and the **Welsh revivals** of 1904–5.
- Individual conversion examples: the **Apostle Paul** and Augustine. C. S. Lewis became convinced of Jesus' divinity after discussions with J. R. R. Tolkien.
- The early 20th-century psychologist and philosopher William James identified several key features believing that they could be viewed as psychologically **positive**, improving one's personal energy.
- Conversions can be **gradual or sudden**; alternatively, a conversion may appear to be sudden, but in actual fact, it may have had a subconscious history for some time prior (i.e. feelings of depression and a growing sense that there may be a God).
- **Types** of conversion can include moving from no religion/atheism to faith (Alister McGrath), from one faith to another faith (Muhammed Ali), from faith-believing to faith-trusting (John Wesley), intellectual (C. S. Lewis) and moral, the cure for a wayward life (Augustine).

Mysticism

- Mysticism is a feature of most religions; it refers to the special experience of **direct access** to the divine realm.
- William James outlined four features of mystical experience: passivity, ineffability, a noetic quality and transiency (**PINT**).
- Passivity refers to the feeling of acceptance and openness; ineffable means defying the ability to describe, noetic refers to achieving special insight and transiency to the temporary or fleeting nature of the experience.
- **Transcendent** means 'rising above'; this can mean rising above and beyond the material world, apprehending a greater reality; other terms to describe this are 'otherworldly' and 'different dimensions'.
- **Rumi**, the 13th-century Muslim poet, believed that what we most love in others is also in our self and, therefore, aspects of God. We can transcend our relationships to find God.
- **Ecstatic** means 'standing outside of oneself', the complete absorption one has in their spiritual awareness. This might be achieved in meditation, dance (the Whirling Dervishes) or other activities.
- Ecstatic experience includes an interior sensation of the mind becoming focused on a subject and a **physical suspension** of the normal activities of the senses – one may appear to be in a trance.
- **Unitive** refers to a sense of unity one has with the divine realm, a removal of the barriers between the self and God (or divine reality).
- A unitive experience includes the sense that everything **exists in God**/divine reality as well as the sense that it is difficult to tell the difference between the deepest levels of ourselves and God/divine reality.

Prayer

- **Teresa of Avila** was a 16th-century Spanish nun, author and leader who established and nurtured many convents.
- For Teresa, the ultimate goal of prayer was **union** with God – she considered that this would involve work and dedication.
- Teresa used the concept of '**stages**' to describe one's progress (through God's grace) to the ultimate goal of prayer. She is noted for using two analogies:

Analogy 1: Watering the Garden

Stage 1: Drawing water from the well. This is the hard work of withdrawing from the outside world, like watering a garden through the work of lifting a bucketful of water from a well.

Stage 2: Using a **winch**. The work of prayer now seems easier, like using a winch to lift the water out of the well. There are fewer distractions; this is the Prayer of Quiet.

Stage 3: Irrigation. Streams are running through the garden and flowers are beginning to bloom. One's soul is saying 'yes' to God.

Stage 4: Heavy **rain**. There is no sense of effort in prayer, the soul is completely enraptured. There is union with God.

Analogy 2: The Interior Castle

Mansions 1–3: the stages prior to union where one: (i) begins to pray, (ii) perseveres in prayer and (iii) where prayer is accompanied by works of love.

Mansion 4: Captivated by God. Here, the soul is completely captivated by God's love. One appears faint or semi-comatose.

Mansion 5: Simple Union. God implants Godself in the soul; after the experience of prayer, it is impossible to doubt that God has been in the soul.

Mansion 6: Spiritual Marriage. There is a sense of rapture, painful longing, spiritual ecstasy and visions.

Mansion 7: Mystical Marriage. The highest level one can attain on earth. One is intuitively and constantly aware of God.

Specification Link

Mysticism – transcendent; ecstatic and unitive.

A religious experience is a subjective sense of perceiving an 'extraordinary' dimension to the world.

❝TRIGGER QUOTES❞

Mysticism has been in the past and probably ever will be one of the great powers of the world. **(W. B. Yeats)**

In this general experience of a unity ... to the world, we have the very inner essence of all mystical experience. **(W. T. Stace)**

God is in all things. The more he is within, the more he remains without. The more he is inside, the more outside. **(Meister Eckhart)**

Specification Link

Prayer – types and stages of prayer according to Teresa of Avila.

❝TRIGGER QUOTES❞

Prayer and comfortable living are incompatible. **(Teresa of Avila)**

Whoever has God lacks nothing; God alone suffices. **(Teresa of Avila)**

The tree that is beside the running water is fresher and gives more fruit. **(Teresa of Avila)**

Let this presence settle into your bones, and allow your soul the freedom to sing, dance, praise and love. **(Teresa of Avila)**

⁶TRIGGER QUOTES⁹

As a result of their experiences many are led to prayer and religion. **(A. Hardy)**

Jesus loves me this I know, for the Bible tells me so. **(popular Christian song)**

One definition of a religious experience is any experience that is given a religious interpretation. **(P. Cole)**

...as this was not an imaginary vision, I could not discern in what form [Jesus was beside me]. **(Teresa of Avila)**

In my daily life everything seemed to be teetering, and my heart needed to be cleansed of the old leaven. **(Augustine)**

If you decide to use a Trigger quote in an exam response, always take time to briefly explain what the quote means and how it fits into your argument.

Issue:

The impact of religious experiences upon religious belief and practice

Three evaluative controversies!

- **Controvery 1:** *Religious experiences do nothing less than birth religions!*
  The **founders** of the world's great religious traditions were each transformed by religious experiences (Moses on Mt Sinai, Jesus in the desert, Muhammad in the cave, Buddha under the Bodhi tree, etc.). Not only this, but these experiences **spawned movements** in which individuals and groups could also have experiences (i.e. the Day of Pentecost, Charismatic churches). However, William James has highlighted the positive psychological value of religious experience. This insight leaves the door open to the argument that what has impacted religion is not 'religious experience' but merely a healthy **psychological experience** – even though that was not James' direct argument.

- **Controvery 2:** *Sacred texts eclipse experience in importance!*
  There is no experience without an interpretation; this interpretation is found in the sacred texts of religion, which provide clear guidelines as to which experiences are '**orthodox**' or 'unorthodox' (leading away from the true faith). Furthermore, these texts spend more time extolling **ethical behaviour** than they do religious experience. For, is not 'love one another' a more important action than seeking to have a vision or mystical experience? Yet, why would one bother studying sacred texts unless the writers had first had an experience of the divine? Furthermore, some religions believe that one must be guided by the divine realm to **interpret texts** effectively (see John 16:13) – is this not an experience?

- **Controvery 3:** *Tradition impacts more than experience!*
  It is difficult if not impossible to pass experiences from **one generation** to another. For, who can replicate the extraordinary visions of Ezekiel, St Paul, Muhammad, Guru Nanak or other special figures? However, traditions can be passed on from one generation to another and are what truly **sustain religions** over time. Traditions also sustain individual believers when they do not have special experiences. Yet, it could be argued that **tradition without experience** is meaningless and the cause of the decline of religion.

Sp⊙tlight: Evaluative judgements

This section contains a special insight that you can use to form a judgement.

The Apostle Paul speaks about love being greater than other spiritual gifts such as healing and speaking in tongues (see I Cor 12 and 13). Similarly, Jesus seemed wary that his followers would become too impressed by miraculous experiences: 'Unless you see signs and wonders you will not believe.' (John 4:48). Does this mean that religious experiences should not be seen as the heart of religion? Or, it could mean merely that 'extraordinary' religious experiences are not the most important aspect of religious belief and practice?

Issue:
Whether different types of religious experience can be accepted as equally valid in communicating religious teachings and beliefs

- **Controvery 1:** *Prayer trumps other experiences!*
  Many religions encourage **learning prayers** as an aspect of reinforcing key beliefs and teachings. For example, in Judaism, the **Shema** is used as a confession of faith. The Lord's prayer is seen by many Christians as the essence of faith; and, for Muslims, daily prayer is one of the five pillars of Islam. Furthermore, visions tend to only be accepted as truth in hindsight, after a figure has been accepted as 'orthodox' in a tradition. On the other hand, the teaching of Teresa of Avila suggests that **prayer is not separate** from visions and mysticism. This is because the aim of the spiritual life is union with God. Furthermore, as many religious traditions do not contain the notion of a single, transcendent God, prayer is not a focus.

- **Controvery 2:** *Conversion is key as it is the gateway to religious beliefs!*
  Some religions teach that one must have a conversion experience before understanding religious beliefs and teachings. Therefore, they emphasise evangelism or **mission** as the foundational experience (for example, the Billy Graham crusades, the Alpha Course and missionaries of Islam such as Ahmad Deedat). However, it could be argued that religious conversion is a central experience only at the **founding** of a religion and that, as time passes, other experiences become more central in the quest to understand religious traditions. For example, **mysticism** could be seen as a later development in Christianity. First, there had to be conversions, such as are described in the book of Acts.

- **Controvery 3:** *Mysticism ushers one into the deepest ways to understand teachings about God/the divine realm!*
  Many religious leaders and writings have pointed out that one needs to go **beyond rational** understanding to attain a knowledge of God/the divine realm. This is best attained through mystical experience (**Teresa of Avila**, Meister Eckhart, John of the Cross, Baal Shem Tov, the Bhagavad Gita 6:7,15,27, Zen Buddhism, etc.). However, there are good reasons why mystics often remain on the 'edge' of their religious traditions: many are unwilling to have their tradition defined by **vague experiences** and believe that God has revealed divine truth through sacred writings.

Can religious experiences be passed on from one generation to another or are traditions and rituals more essential for the survival of a religion?

Sp🔘tlight: Evaluative judgements
This section contains a special insight that you can use to form a judgement.

One feature of mystical experience, according to William James, is 'ineffability', the notion that such an experience cannot be conveyed by words. This certainly puts a limitation on this kind of experience for communicating religious beliefs to anyone other than the subject. On the other hand, James said that mystical experiences often had a 'noetic' quality – a sense that one had gained knowledge of the divine. This has led many mystics to describe their experiences and, thus, their beliefs about the nature of God.

Quick Revision
One way to save time in preparing for an exam is to focus only on the religion you are studying as the basis for examples you can apply to these issues. Jot down the name of some traditions within the religion you are studying. Beside the name of each tradition write down which kinds of religious experiences are considered to be more – and less – important … and why.

AO1 Trigger revision activity

A ZIP

Visions and conversion

visions	intellectual content	Welsh revivals
beyond normal	groups and individuals	Apostle Paul
features	Guru Nanak	positive
sensory	turning around	gradual or sudden
dream	collective or individual	types

1 Here is your zip file of portable Triggers.

2 Practise 'downloading' your zip file of Triggers from memory. See how many you can recall on first attempt.

3 When you are confident enough, order the Triggers into a list as you may do in an examination situation.

Why Trigger?
Remember, your Triggers are to help you transfer your knowledge and understanding in a manageable, efficient and portable manner.

TIP

5 Now read through your descriptions and think about ways in which you could develop these using your Trigger quotes.

4 Attempt to write one clear sentence to define each Trigger.

B ZIP

Mysticism and prayer

Mysticism	Prayer
exists in God	winch
unitive	union
transcendent	Mystical marriage
Rumi	Simple Union
physical suspension	drawing water
direct access	irrigation
	rain
	Teresa of Avila
	Mansions 1-3
	captivated
	Spiritual marriage
	watering the garden

1 Fix the zip file! There are four Triggers missing from this zip file – find them and add them in.

2 There's another problem: the Triggers are out of order! Put them in the same order as they appear in the AO1 section above.

6 Now read through your definitions and think about ways in which you could develop these using your Trigger quotes.

3 Practise 'downloading' your zip file of Triggers from memory. See how many you can recall on first attempt.

5 Attempt to write one clear sentence to define each Trigger.

4 When you are confident enough, order the Triggers into a list as you may do in an examination situation.

AO2 Trigger revision activity

A   ZIP

The impact of religious experiences upon religious belief and practice

Birth religions!
founders, spawned movements, psychological experience

Sacred texts eclipse!
orthodox, ethical behaviour, interpret texts

Tradition impacts!
one generation, sustain religions, tradition without experience

1 Here is your zip file of portable Triggers.

2 Practise 'downloading' your zip file of Triggers from memory. See how many you can recall on first attempt.

3 When you are confident enough, order the Triggers into a list as you may do in an examination situation.

5 Now read through all your sentences and think about ways in which you could develop these using your Trigger quotes, further examples, and noting strengths and weaknesses.

4 'Double-click' each Trigger in your memory – what can you say about an evaluative point of view in a clear sentence? Write this down. Do this for each Trigger in turn.

REVISION TIP

Using Trigger quotes
When you choose the Trigger quotes that you wish to use make sure that you explain how they are relevant.

B   ZIP

Views on the nature of God impacting arguments

Mysticism ushers,
beyond rational, Teresa of Avila

Prayer trumps, learning
prayers, prayer is not separate

Conversion is key!
founding, mysticism

1 Fix the zip file! There are three Triggers missing from this zip file – find them and add them in.

2 There's another problem: the Triggers are out of order! Put them in the same order as they appear in the AO2 section above.

3 Practise 'downloading' your zip file of Triggers from memory. See how many you can recall on first attempt.

6 Now read through all your sentences and think about ways in which you could develop these using your Trigger quotes, further examples, and noting strengths and weaknesses.

5 Attempt to write one clear sentence to define each Trigger.

4 When you are confident enough, order the Triggers into a list as you may do in an examination situation.

Specification Link

Visions – sensory; intellectual; dreams.

AO1

**What is ...
Knowledge and
understanding ?**

This is the skill that involves *selecting* the relevant and appropriate information, *organising* it and then *presenting* it through a *personal explanation* that may involve the use of supporting *evidence* and *examples*.

Spot the Triggers!
The words in blue are Triggers – key words and phrases that can help you remember knowledge and understanding in this area.

TIP

🎵 TRIGGER QUOTES 🎵

Passivity ... the mystic feels as if his own will were in abeyance. **(W. James)**

Ineffability ... it defies expression, that no adequate report of its contents can be given in words. **(W. James)**

Noetic quality ... mystical states seem to those who experience them to be also states of knowledge. **(W. James)**

Transiency ... mystical states cannot be sustained for long. **(W. James)**

Theme 4B: Mystical experience

William James

- William James (b. 1842) was an American philosopher and psychologist who provided an account of mystical experience in his book the *Varieties of Religious Experience*.
- His view was that though mystical experiences were beyond the realm of empirical science, they **transformed** the lives of the recipients in a positive way.
- Mystical experiences speak to religious sentiments such as the ideal, vastness, **union**, safety and rest.
- James classified mystical experience into four categories: passivity, ineffability, noetic quality and transiency (**PINT**).
- **Passivity** refers to the fact that though one might make preparations for a mystical experience (concentration, physical positions, etc.), once the experience has begun, the mystic feels 'grasped' by a superior power. In the passive state, the mystic may manifest a **secondary personality** through prophetic speech, automatic writing or having a trance state.
- **Ineffability** is the sense that the mystical experience cannot be put into words; it is a direct experience. Just as no one can make it clear to another that they have had a certain, highly important feeling, the mystic feels that they **cannot convey** the depth of their experience.
- The **noetic quality** of a mystical experience is the sense that one has gained a state of knowledge. This is a **state of insight** where one believes they have encountered illumination or a revelation of great significance.
- **Transiency** refers to the fact that mystical states cannot be sustained for long; they are intense, but fleeting.
- James believes the limits of the mystical experience are, at most, **an hour or two** – but often they are much shorter than this.

Quick Revision

Read Isaiah 6 and make a list of the Trigger words from William James that are relevant to this experience. Make a second list of Trigger words from Rudolph Otto that are relevant. Find a second example of a religious experience from the religion you are studying and do the same. This will help you respond to an exam question asking you to describe these theories.

The term 'passive' often has negative and unhealthy associations, such as 'passive smoke'. Yet, for James, passivity is a key (and healthy) characteristic of the mystical experience.

Rudolph Otto

- Rudolph Otto was a **German protestant** theologian who believed that the study of religion had focused too exclusively on the rational and intellectual development of beliefs.
- Otto pointed out that religions are based on founders having had powerful encounters with God in which feelings and **non-rational** elements are central.
- His book, *The Idea of the Holy*, focuses on the **sense of power** that accompanies religious experience.
- Otto used the term **numinous** to describe these experiences, from the Latin term, 'numen' ('divine power').
- The numinous is not an intellectual experience with 'truth', 'beauty' or 'morality' in religion. It is an experience of the **awesome** power of God.
- A numinous experience can be gentle or sudden and powerful. It can even **repel and fascinate** at the same time.
- Otto used the Latin phrase ***mysterium tremendum et fascinans***: an 'Other' who we discover is both tremendous and fascinating – it refers to the dual experience of both the power and attractiveness of God.
- Otto felt that fear (as in awe) of God and the love of God were **two sides** of the same experience.
- As was common in his context, he believed that Christianity was the **most advanced** religion.
- However, he believed this not because of its rational doctrines, but because it provided the perfect type of numinous experience, a **balance** between fear/awe of God and love of God.

Specification Link

Rudolf Otto—the concept of the numinous; mysterium tremendum; the human predisposition for religious experience.

❛TRIGGER QUOTES❜

'the holy' ... contains a quite specific element or 'moment' which sets it apart from 'The Rational'. **(R. Otto)**

The mysterium is the wholly-other, an object eluding all understanding. It ... fills the mind with 'wonder and astonishment'. **(R. Otto)**

The tremendum, the daunting and repelling moment of the numinous ... **(R. Otto)**

The fascinans, the attracting and alluring moment of the numinous ... **(R. Otto)**

Rudolph Otto objected to a study of religion focusing only on ideas, doctrines, beliefs and moral positions. After all, the founders of religions had an experience that defies being understood in only rational terms.

AO2

What is ... Evaluation and critical analysis ?

The AO2 skills of evaluation and critical analysis mean engaging with the controversies surrounding a subject. This is more than merely describing or listing the points made about a controversy. To achieve this, one weighs up strengths and weaknesses of various sides and takes a position. On the right are three controversies for each issue – you can engage in these by extending their arguments (adding examples, quotes or other details), weighing up their strengths and weaknesses, and coming to a conclusion.

❛TRIGGER QUOTES❜

He (James) is vulnerable to charges like that of side-lining historical context. **(M. Vernon)**

The phenomena of mystical experience may occur outside the framework of any formal religion with no reference to an articulated theology. **(P. Cole)**

... the experience itself ... is shaped by concepts which the mystic brings to, and which shape, his experience. **(S. Katz)**

Quick Revision

Choose one religious experience from the religion you are studying and make three lists: (i) elements in this experience that correspond to James' categories, (ii) elements in this experience that correspond to Otto's key ideas, (iii) elements of this experience that could be unique to the cultural context of the 'experiencer' (i.e. history, language, geography). This will help you to make critical comparisons on an exam evaluation question.

Issue:

The adequacy of James' four characteristics in defining mystical experience

Three evaluative controversies!

- **Controversy 1: *James' characteristics are not objective!***
  James uses **literary sources** rather than an interview approach to his work – this includes famous examples mainly from the **Christian tradition** (including Teresa of Avila) and contemporary Western sources. Thus, it could be said that by his **editorial choices** he is shaping the very thing he wishes to define rather than attempting to really see if there is a universal phenomenon to which his ideas relate. However, James does refer to other religions in his book and his ideas have been respected for over a century, acknowledged by many who have studied mystical phenomena (F. C. Happold, N. Smart and others).

- **Controversy 2: *He leaves out the most common mystical experience!***
  It is surprising that James omits from his main characteristics the one quality of the experience which so many mystics seek, find and testify to: the sense of **union or oneness** (Meister Eckhart, Teresa of Avila, St Catherine of Genoa, etc.). In fact, the sense of achieving oneness with everything was proposed as one of three additions to James' categories by **F. C. Happold** (along with a sense of timelessness and the understanding that the ego is not the real 'I'). On the other hand, it could be argued that the sense of union or oneness is just one aspect of James' **'noetic quality'**. In fact, James' categorisation is made more universal by not reporting on the actual insights reached by those with a mystical experience.

- **Controversy 3: *Any classification is doomed!***
  James' **assumption** seems to be that mysticism is a universal phenomenon with universal categories. However, not only are his sources limited, but it could be argued that he has failed to recognise the role that religious and **cultural contexts** play in defining experiences. This means that whilst his categories might work for many '**Western**' and monotheistic experiences, those from other cultures or religions might not make sense of them. For instance, some Buddhist traditions seek 'emptiness' or 'nothingness' for which terms such as noetic, ineffable, transient and passive may be irrelevant.

Spotlight: Evaluative judgements

This section contains a special insight that you can use to form a judgement.

William James examines mysticism from an individual rather than a collective point of view. Is this really possible? Peter Cole, in his book *Religious Experience*, notes the view of Stephen Katz who says that there is no such thing as a 'pure experience' – we can never untangle an experience from its historical, linguistic, geographical (etc.) settings. If Katz is right, then it makes James' approach a dubious enterprise.

Issue:
The adequacy of Otto's definition of 'numinous'.

- **Controversy 1:** *Religions are reduced to a feeling by Otto!*
  Otto's approach countered those who wanted to reduce religion to doctrines, morality or aesthetics – all rational concepts. However, is not Otto guilty of a reduction? For he insists that the deepest element of religion is an **emotion** that evokes both awe and fascination (mysterium tremendum et fascinans), even saying that this is an '**a priori**' category in the human species. Would it not be better to see religion as **multi-dimensional**? That is, religion includes emotions such as those Otto describes – as well as doctrine, ethics, architecture (etc.). None of these are more important or fundamental than the others.

- **Controversy 2:** *'The Holy' is too vague to have meaning!*
  Otto believes that all religious experience stems from a sense of the 'holy', for which he uses the term '**numinous**' (from Lat. 'numen', meaning divinity). He says that there are both crude and more refined expressions of the numinous ranging from terror at unseen forces to awe in the face of a mysterious 'other'. Yet, what does all of this really mean? Firstly, 'holy' and 'numinous' are vague terms which could be identified with even **contradictory** views of God/the divine realm. Secondly, the range of experiences which could fit into Otto's category are almost endless; this makes 'the numinous' **too broad** a category to be helpful.

- **Controversy 3:** *Otto makes religion impersonal!*
  Otto focuses on the '**otherness**' of God and the feelings of awe and fascination that one has in the face of this tremendous mystery (mysterium tremendum). Yet, are there not many who experience religion differently? Instead of 'Otherness' many find a sense of '**relatedness**' with the divine realm which they would describe as 'personal' rather than 'impersonal'. For instance, the Jewish philosopher **Martin Buber** says that we encounter God in personal relationships – which he describes as 'I-thou' rather than the impersonal 'I-it'.

The sense of awe or healthy fear we might have in the face of a potentially dangerous but beautiful natural phenomenon captures Otto's 'mysterium tremendum et fascinans'.

❛TRIGGER QUOTES❜

The numinous...issues from the deepest foundation of cognitive apprehension that the soul possesses. **(R. Otto)**

... we come upon something inherently 'wholly other', whose kind and character are incommensurable with our own ... **(R. Otto)**

And Moses hid his face, for he was afraid to look at God. **(Exodus 3:6)**

When two people relate to each other authentically and humanly, God is the electricity that surges between them.
(Martin Buber)

Sp⬤tlight: Evaluative judgements
This section contains a special insight that you can use to form a judgement.

Rudolph Otto raises a valuable idea: how can we consider studying a religion without exploring the importance of its non-rational aspects? Take a look at the specification outline for the religion you are studying – do you think Otto would say that the feelings of awe, fear and fascination have been a focus of your studies? Or would he conclude that religion was being reduced by WJEC/Eduqas to its rational aspects of doctrine, beliefs, morality, philosophy and aesthetics?

TIP

When you use Trigger quotes in an evaluative response, make sure that you explain how they are relevant.

AO1 Trigger revision activity

A ZIP

William James

Varieties of Secular Experience

transformed

union

QUART

passivity

secondary personality

ineffability

compelling

noetic quality

state of insight

permanent

splendid

1 Find the unhelpful Triggers! **This zip file contains several inappropriate or irrelevant Triggers**. Find these and replace them with the real Triggers from the AO1 section.

→

2 There's another problem: the Triggers are out of order! Put them in the same order as they appear in the AO1 section above.

→

3 Practise 'downloading' your zip file of Triggers from memory. See how many you can recall on first attempt.

6 Now read through your definitions and think about ways in which you could develop these using your Trigger quotes.

←

5 Attempt to write one clear sentence to define each Trigger.

←

4 When you are confident enough, order the Triggers into a list as you may do in an examination situation.

B ZIP

Rudolph Otto

German protestant

non-rational

sense of power

numinous

awesome

repel and fascinate

mysterium tremendum et fascinans

two sides

most advanced

balance

1 Here is your zip file of portable Triggers.

→

2 Practise 'downloading' your zip file of Triggers from memory. See how many you can recall on first attempt.

→

3 When you are confident enough, order the Triggers into a list as you may do in an examination situation.

Why Trigger?
Remember, your Triggers are to help you transfer your knowledge and understanding in a manageable, efficient and portable manner.

TIP

5 Now read through your descriptions and think about ways in which you could develop these using your Trigger quotes.

←

4 Attempt to write one clear sentence to define each Trigger.

AO2 Trigger revision activity

 A **ZIP**

The adequacy of James' four characteristics in defining mystical experience

not objective, literary sources, Rastafarianism, editorial choices.	classification is doomed! James' assumption, cultural contexts, Australian	leaves out, union or oneness, F. C. Happold, humorous quality

1 Find the unhelpful Triggers! **This zip file contains several inappropriate or irrelevant Triggers**. Find these and replace them with the real Triggers from the AO2 section.

2 There's another problem: the Triggers are out of order! Put them in the same order as they appear in the AO2 section above.

3 Practise 'downloading' your zip file of Triggers from memory. See how many you can recall on first attempt.

6 Now read through all your sentences and think about ways in which you could develop these using your Trigger quotes, further examples, and noting strengths and weaknesses.

5 Attempt to write one clear sentence to define each Trigger.

4 When you are confident enough, order the Triggers into a list as you may do in an examination situation.

 B **ZIP**

The adequacy of Otto's definition of 'numinous'

Religions are reduced! emotion, a priori, multi-dimensional	too vague, numinous, contradictory, too broad	impersonal! otherness, relatedness, Martin Buber

1 Here is your zip file of portable Triggers.

2 Practise 'downloading' your zip file of Triggers from memory. See how many you can recall on first attempt.

3 When you are confident enough, order the Triggers into a list as you may do in an examination situation.

5 Now read through all your sentences and think about ways in which you could develop these using your Trigger quotes, further examples, and noting strengths and weaknesses.

4 'Double-click' each Trigger in your memory – what can you say about an evaluative point of view in a clear sentence? Write this down. Do this for each Trigger in turn.

REVISION TIP

Using Trigger quotes
When you choose the Trigger quotes that you wish to use make sure that you explain how they are relevant.

Theme 4C: Challenges to the objectivity and authenticity of religious experience

Challenges to religious experiences

AO1

What is ... Knowledge and understanding **?**

This is the skill that involves *selecting* the relevant and appropriate information, *organising* it and then *presenting* it through a *personal explanation* that may involve the use of supporting *evidence* and *examples*.

Spot the Triggers!
The words in blue are Triggers – key words and phrases that can help you remember knowledge and understanding in this area.

TIP

⁶TRIGGER QUOTES⁹

Religious experiences are not the sort of thing which can easily be produced for observation in a controlled setting. **(C. Franks Davis)**

Auto-descriptions of subjects' experiences may be rejected as evidence if the subjects are known to be pathological liars ... **(C. Franks Davis)**

Subject-related challenges are thus most damaging when we have no independent access to the putative object of the experience ... **(C. Franks Davis)**

- Many reports of religious experiences (REs) are **individualistic** and subjective in nature and therefore not open to rational enquiry.
- The **inconsistency** of REs with everyday life is another reason to question their authenticity.
- Those who challenge REs believe that if the subject had more **scientific knowledge**, self-awareness and/or linguistic precision they would abandon their claims.
- Caroline Franks Davis categorises all challenges into **three categories**: description-related, subject-related and object-related.
- **Description challenges** involve misremembering, exaggerating, misusing terms or telling lies. An example of a description challenge is a **highly interpreted** description ('I had an experience of the Holy Trinity, Father, Son and Holy Spirit'), which may be a ground for doubt.
- **Subject challenges** centre on the unreliability, impairment or moral laxity of the subjects claiming REs. Common subject-related challenges include the experience having occurred in a state of sleep, hypnosis, **intoxication**, loneliness, fear (or other psychological/physiological state).
- **Object challenges** centre on the implausibility of the object of the experience existing and/or having been the cause of the experience. Object challenges include attacks on the traditional inductive and deductive **arguments for God** (i.e. design, ontological, etc.)
- The most common subject-related arguments include the **reduction** of REs to psychological, sociological or anthropological factors.
- Examples include Freud's reduction of RE to sexual repression, Émile Durkheim's insight that society is God and anthropologist **Ioan Lewis'** insight of REs being related to the need of individuals to access social or political power in a pre-industrial setting.

- The **conflicting-claims** argument (also a subject-related challenge) focuses on the differences of claims between religions: they can't all be right.

Would you trust this person's report of a religious experience? Intoxication is one of many subject-related challenges according to Caroline Franks Davis.

Defending religious experience

- Caroline **Franks Davis defends** REs against these challenges.
- Description-related challenges are minimised because those with REs are trying to describe something beyond normal experience – therefore one should not expect **linguistic precision**.
- Furthermore, those with highly interpreted experiences are often willing to speak about their experience without their usual **interpretation**.
- With subject-related challenges, someone can be **impaired** and yet report an event accurately – therefore these must not be summarily dismissed.
- With object-related challenges, there are many arguments for God; they never claim to be the only way to prove God. They are a part of a **larger picture**.
- Franks Davis appeals to three principles from **Richard Swinburne**: credulity, testimony and cumulative strength.
- Credulity has to do with accepting our (and others') sense experience as valid. Otherwise we would be lost in a **'sceptical bog'**. There are limitations to sense experience, but we should at least begin an investigation with **openness** or credulity.
- The principle of **testimony** asserts that we live our lives, in large part, by trusting the testimony of others. We can't check on everything we are told; we must accept that, unless there are grounds for doubting, people normally tell the **truth**.
- The **cumulative argument** asks skeptics to consider the combined power of REs all over the world coupled with arguments for God. This pushes RE from the 'improbable' to the 'probable'.

Specification Link

Challenges: individual experiences valid even if non-verifiable; claims could be genuine – integrity of individual; one-off experiences can still be valid even if never repeated.

Quick Revision

Make a list of all of the possible objections you can think of to reports of religious experiences. Then, beside each objection write which challenge (description, subject or object) fits best. Ensure you have a few examples of each type – you can use these to help you explain the meaning of these challenges for an AO1 exam question.

❝TRIGGER QUOTES❞

These principles of credulity and testimony are ultimate principles of rationality which ally to all types of perceptual experience …
(C. Franks Davis)

The fact that so many religious experiences have beneficial consequences is some evidence in their favour. This is the 'fruits' argument …
(C. Franks Davis)

TIP

Remember, your Triggers are to help you transfer your knowledge and understanding in a manageable, efficient and portable manner.

According to Franks Davis and Swinburne, a good case for religious experience builds up when one looks at the cumulative evidence of religious experience along with arguments for God.

What is ... Evaluation and critical analysis ?

The AO2 skills of evaluation and critical analysis mean engaging with the controversies surrounding a subject. This is more than merely describing or listing the points made about a controversy. To achieve this, one weighs up strengths and weaknesses of various sides and takes a position. On the right are three controversies for each issue – you can engage in these by extending their arguments (adding examples, quotes or other details), weighing up their strengths and weaknesses, and coming to a conclusion.

⁶TRIGGER QUOTES⁹

Religion is an illusion and it derives its strength from the fact that it falls in with our instinctual desires. **(S. Freud)**

... religious force is nothing but the collective and anonymous force of the clan ... **(E. Durkheim)**

... a Catholic, for instance, is more likely to see Mary, a Protestant will see Christ, a Muslim, of course, Allah. **(R. Persinger)**

Quick Revision

If someone reported a religious experience to you which you felt was questionable, which one of the three types of objection would you use? Now write a paragraph defending your scepticism and then a paragraph criticising your scepticism – use Trigger words from this subtheme.

Issue:

The extent to which the challenges to religious experience are valid

Three evaluative controversies!

☐ **Controversy 1: *'Sense' is not sensory!***
Many claim that their REs involve a sense of sight, hearing, smell or touch. However, this is not the same as having an **observable**, repeatable sensory experience which can be tested. The experimental method is our only way to determine truth from falsehood. The fact that this method cannot be applied to REs makes them suspect. **Logical positivists** argue that a claim for truth (other than a logical tautology) not based on sense experience is, simply, nonsense. However, there are some REs that are **communally experienced** (Angel of Mons, Charismatic phenomena). These provide multiple sensory attestations to the same experience.

☐ **Controversy 2: *There are materialistic explanations!***
The fascinating area of neuroscience has located REs in different areas of the brain, including the **frontal lobes**. These experiences can be stimulated by drugs or magnetic fields (such as the **Persinger helmet**). This means that REs can be created and are therefore natural rather than supernatural experiences. However, it could be argued that these stimulations of the human brain actually allow it easy access to a 'reality' that is already present. In other words, the brain is not the sole cause of these experiences, but merely a **conduit**.

☐ **Controversy 3: *A cumulative argument!***
Swinburne and Franks Davis argue that the sheer number of REs across the world combined with the many philosophical arguments for God produce a strong 'cumulative case'. However, is there not also a cumulative case against REs? This case is composed of explanations from the **fields** of psychology (S. Freud), sociology (E. Durkheim), anthropology (I. Lewis), neuroscience and brain research – along with the many reasons for valid **suspicion** of **auto-reporting** of experience and the many challenges to the traditional arguments for God. The effect of all of these objections is a cumulative case against REs.

Spotlight: **Evaluative judgements**

This section contains a special insight that you can use to form a judgement.

The conflicting claims challenge is one of many subject-related challenges to REs. It has to do with a great many people saying that they have experienced some object or event but giving wholly different accounts of it. This could be because they are lying, misremembering, or using different interpretations. One aspect of the conflicting claims argument is the fact that many religions cannot agree on the essential aspects of religious experience. This is an epistemic failure and we are therefore right to be suspicious of any report of an RE.

Issue:

The persuasiveness of Franks Davis' different challenges

■ **Controversy 1:** *Faulty descriptions* **are not a problem!**

It can easily be shown that many reports of REs use **imprecise** terms, have inconsistencies with similar reports and are presented in a highly interpreted way, thus showing the predisposition of the subject to their experience. However, Franks Davis points out that all of this is exactly what we would expect if a person really were having a **unique experience** which fell outside of all other events in their lives. We would expect them to 'reach' for language in a way that wasn't accurate. Therefore, we should keep an **open mind** when coming across description challenges in the reporting of REs.

■ **Controversy 2:** *It's possible to be* **over-sceptical** *with subjects!*

There are numerous ways to cast doubt on those who report REs from intoxication and lazy thinking to psychological, sociological and cultural predispositions to believe in the reality of these experiences. The result of all of these subject-challenges can be to label all subjects of REs as **mentally deficient**, unenlightened and, therefore, untrustworthy. Yet, it is a well-known fact that many honest, **intelligent** and moral human beings have religious experiences. When this fact is combined with Swinburne's principles of **credulity and testimony**, keeping an open mind to the subjects of REs, especially when subjects are known to be trustworthy and intelligent human beings, would seem to be the best approach.

■ **Controversy 3:** *Get* **beyond the detail** *with the object of REs!*

There are a number of valid ways to object to Aquinas' Five Ways, the ontological argument or more modern restatements of arguments from design. These are object-related challenges according to Franks Davis. The usual thinking is that when a 'hole' can be picked in an argument for God's existence, the entire argument **crumbles**. However, both Franks Davis and Richard Swinburne believe that focusing on the detail of these arguments can be **short-sighted**, missing the significance of the **sheer number** of arguments for God. Does not the fact that there are so many arguments bear witness to the reality of an object to human religious experience?

Many descriptions of REs may 'miss the mark' in terms of linguistic precision or correspondence to descriptions of other REs. But isn't this to be expected of a description of an extraordinary experience?

Quick Revision

Choose one point from Franks Davis in favour of the validity of religious experience. Whether or not you agree with her point, extend it by adding quotes and examples. Then, write down the best arguments (along with quotes, examples and scholars) against this. Repeat this exercise with her other points – and you will be well on your way for an exam evaluation question in this area.

S●tlight: Evaluative judgements

This section contains a special insight that you can use to form a judgement.

We may be quick to dismiss a RE in a dream or hallucinatory state as a route to knowledge of the supernatural. Yet, Franks Davis notes that in the secular realm dreams, visions and flashes of insight have been proven to lead to knowledge. For example, there are accounts of scientists (such as August Kekulé) who received solutions to scientific challenges in dreams or upon waking from sleep. This should be enough to treat REs in dreams, visions and hallucinations as innocent until proven guilty.

❛TRIGGER QUOTES❜

[Religious individuals] are challenged on all sides, by philosophers, psychologists, sociologists ... and even by members of their own tradition .... **(C. Franks Davis)**

Where such [subject] challenges are successful, it is still possible that the experience in question was veridical. **(C. Franks Davis)**

Cumulative cases ... can appeal to a wide range of evidence. **(C. Franks Davis)**

AO1 Trigger revision activity

A

Challenges to religious experiences

1 There are no Triggers in this zip file! Find and add in the relevant Triggers.

2 Now put the Triggers in the same order as they appear in the AO1 section above.

3 Practise 'downloading' your zip file of Triggers from memory. See how many you can recall on first attempt.

6 Now read through your definitions and think about ways in which you could develop these using your Trigger quotes.

5 Attempt to write one clear sentence to define each Trigger.

4 When you are confident enough, order the Triggers into a list as you may do in an examination situation.

B

Defending religious experience

Franks Davis defends	**art gallery**	**testimony**
measurement	**Richard Swinburne**	**journalistic**
Boolean logic	**sceptical bog**	**cumulative argument**
impaired	**openness**	

1 Find the unhelpful Triggers! **This zip file contains several inappropriate or irrelevant Triggers**. Find these and replace them with the real Triggers from the AO1 section.

2 There's another problem: the Triggers are out of order! Put them in the same order as they appear in the AO1 section above.

3 Practise 'downloading' your zip file of Triggers from memory. See how many you can recall on first attempt.

6 Now read through your definitions and think about ways in which you could develop these using your Trigger quotes.

5 Attempt to write one clear sentence to define each Trigger.

4 When you are confident enough, order the Triggers into a list as you may do in an examination situation.

AO2 Trigger revision activity

A

ZIP

Challenges to RE as valid

1 There are no Triggers in this zip file! Find and add in the relevant Triggers.

2 Now put the Triggers in the same order as they appear in the AO2 section above.

3 Practise 'downloading' your zip file of Triggers from memory. See how many you can recall on first attempt.

6 Now read through all your sentences and think about ways in which you could develop these using your Trigger quotes, further examples, and noting strengths and weaknesses.

5 Attempt to write one clear sentence to define each Trigger.

4 When you are confident enough, order the Triggers into a list as you may do in an examination situation.

B

ZIP

Persuasiveness of Franks Davis' different challenges

Beyond the detail, Philo, short-sighted, sheer number	Over-sceptical, mentally deficient, intelligent, investigation	Faulty descriptions, imprecise, psychedelic, open mind

1 Find the unhelpful Triggers! **This zip file contains several inappropriate or irrelevant Triggers**. Find these and replace them with the real Triggers from the AO2 section.

2 There's another problem: the Triggers are out of order! Put them in the same order as they appear in the AO2 section above.

3 Practise 'downloading' your zip file of Triggers from memory. See how many you can recall on first attempt.

6 Now read through all your sentences and think about ways in which you could develop these using your Trigger quotes, further examples, and noting strengths and weaknesses.

5 Attempt to write one clear sentence to define each Trigger.

4 When you are confident enough, order the Triggers into a list as you may do in an examination situation.

Using Triggers to create exam answers

Below you will find answers for sample AO1 and AO2 questions in each theme. The Triggers have been highlighted so that you can see how these have been used to form an answer to a possible exam question.

> Comments in the margins of these pages will give you added insights on qualities of an effective answer.

T1: Some areas for examination

An answer using the Triggers to assist in explaining different versions of the cosmological argument.

> Each paragraph is focused on exactly what has been asked.

Thomas Aquinas demonstrated five ways to prove the existence of God. Despite the fact that the moral and design arguments are cosmological in nature, the first three of Aquinas' ways are traditionally referred to as the cosmological argument. Aquinas bases his arguments on observation of how the 'cosmos' functions and then draws the conclusion that for the universe to function as it does then there must have been a divine originator. The argument is **inductive**, which means it is based on reasoning that leads to a **probable** conclusion.

This theory he applies to change or motion, cause and contingency in the following ways. Since things in the world are in motion or experience change then they must have been moved by something else; an infinite regress of movements is impossible so there must be a first mover, which is God.

In the same way, there is no one thing in the world that could have caused itself because this would mean that it existed prior to itself; therefore, since an infinite regress of causes is impossible, there must have been a first cause, which is God.

> No judgement has been made as to the validity of the argument as this would not be appropriate for an 'explain' question/AO1 response.

Finally, since things in the world are **contingent** (that is they came into existence and there will be a time when they cease to exist) then there must have been a time when nothing existed; therefore, unless the universe had an external and eternal cause (necessary) then there would be nothing here now – as we are here now then the **necessary** cause of the universe must be God. This is also the reason why there can be no **infinite regress** of movement, causes or beings.

The **Kalam** argument is based in an Arabic term meaning 'argue' or 'discuss' and was introduced by Muslim scholars al-Kindi and al-Ghazali. It was later developed by scholars such as William Craig in the 20th century. Craig first makes the distinction between a potentially infinite and actually infinite universe.

According to Craig, an actually infinite universe could have nothing added to it because it is already infinite (this reflects the mathematical understanding of the concept of infinity) and therefore we could have no past, present or future. Such a mathematical concept has no meaning or relevance to our empirical world.

Instead, Craig offers a more practical, empirical understanding of a **potentially infinite** universe whereby one can always add to this. However, if the past did not have a beginning then it must be **actually infinite** (not potentially) but that would mean that the future would be the same as the past because even if things were added then they would make no difference, and this is illogical; therefore, the past cannot even be potentially infinite and must have a beginning.

This beginning must have been caused by God – but why? Since the universe was caused rather than uncaused, then it was either a natural occurrence or through choice or will. As the rules of nature did not exist before the universe then it cannot be the result of natural causes and must have been brought into existence by a personal being who chose this to be so. He appeals to the idea of a personal God as a link between the finite and infinite realms, as he says, 'I think that it can be plausibly argued that the cause of the universe must be a personal Creator. For how else could a temporal effect arise from an eternal cause?'

> A number of specialist terms have been used throughout this response.

> A Trigger quote has been used to strengthen this response.

Evaluating, and utilising the associated Triggers for, the specific controversy over the effectiveness of challenges to Aquinas' cosmological argument.

AO2

Aquinas' first three ways are **empirical** arguments, based in experience and observation (a posteriori) and draw conclusions based upon this that are **contingent**; that is, the arguments are dependent upon the first observation being true or alternatively, it is the case that the conclusion does not necessarily follow from the premise. In this way, they cannot logically prove anything but serve to act as 'proof' in so far as making something highly probable at best.

Hume challenges the cosmological argument by suggesting the whole notion of causality is limited to things that begin to exist. If the universe is eternal or infinite, then the question about cause is irrelevant: 'I would say it is just there and that is all' is his famous response when questioned about cause.

> This paragraph ends with a 'mini-conclusion'; this demonstrates evaluative ability.

> Relevant use of Trigger quote.

The Trigger quote used in this paragraph is from the AO1 section – candidates should use any Triggers or Trigger quotes that help them answer the question.

This answer effectively refers to the 'controversies' covered in the Evaluation section.

There is a clear conclusion that flows from points made earlier.

Hume also presented what later came to be known as the fallacy of composition. An observed cause and effect within the universe does not mean that this rule applies to the universe collectively and as a whole. Russell used the example, 'Just because every human has a mother does not mean the whole of humanity has a mother.' Hume believed that when we explain every part of the universe, we are in fact explaining the whole.

Finally, Hume argued that we can only be certain about the things we experience and have no experience of creating a universe. Therefore, there is not enough evidence either for a first cause for the universe and what the cause might have been.

Hume's arguments are seen to be effective by many and we can confidently argue that in philosophical circles the cosmological argument has been firmly challenged. In particular, the illogical step of actually seeking out a First Cause has been taken up by Russell and others. Nonetheless, Hume's view concerning causes is not universally accepted. Even when one event follows another, we distinguish between the ideas both of cause and coincidence. This, then, suggests they are different things. In addition, Richard Swinburne also pointed out that the existence of an observer has no bearing on the probability of the occurrence of the events being observed. What needs explaining is the occurrence of the event, not the fact that we have been able to experience the event first hand. In relation to the question, this does not mean that the argument is an impossibility or that philosophy has rejected the proposals outright. Craig has also demonstrated that there are aspects of the cosmological argument that have relevance today.

Nevertheless, those who argue for the cosmological argument and defend Aquinas and Craig can only at best admit stalemate. In this way, I must argue that whilst a remote possibility of the argument being the case has to be admitted, it does not make the argument strong enough to be considered more probable than its counterpart and I therefore agree with the statement.

T2: **Some areas for examination**

An answer using the Triggers to assist in explaining Norman Malcolm's view of the ontological argument.

Norman Malcolm, a 20th-century philosopher, is in favour of the ontological argument. However, he **rejects** Anselm's argument in Proslogion 2 which attempts to define God (defined as 'that-than-which-nothing-greater-can-be-conceived') into existence based on the supposed fact that it is better to exist in reality than to only exist in the mind. Malcolm appears to echo **Kant's** criticism that existence cannot be a predicate, as it tells us nothing about the concept. An '**insulated house**', Malcolm says, is better than an 'uninsulated house'; it does not make sense to say that an 'existing house' is better than a 'non-existing house'.

> Each paragraph is focused on exactly what has been asked.

However, Malcolm does see merit in Anselm's discussion of the **necessary existence** of God in Proslogion 3. Malcolm expresses the concept of necessary existence of God as an **unlimited being**. This quality of being unlimited must apply to not only God's actions, but God's existence. This is a meaningful concept when describing God. This leads Malcolm to an argument for God which can be expressed in this way:

Premise 1: Anselm's definition of God as 'that-than-which-nothing-greater-can-be-conceived' is a **logically sound description** of an unlimited being.

> No judgement has been made as to the validity of Malcolm's approach as this would not be appropriate for an 'explain' question/AO1 response.

Premise 2: An unlimited being **cannot come into existence**, for this would mean that he was caused to exist or just happened to exist – each qualities of limited beings.

Premise 3: An unlimited being **cannot cease existing**, as this would also be the quality of a limited being.

This leads to the conclusion that, as Malcolm says, 'His [God's] existence must either be logically **necessary** or logically **impossible**'. This means that there is no 'middle ground' when it comes to the existence of God. Malcolm states that since the definition for God which he provided is logically sound, then God's exists is logically necessary and not logically impossible. Malcolm's argument, then, is a development of the ontological argument following an aspect of Anselm's concept of God as a necessary being.

> Note the effective use of a short Trigger quote along with a brief explanation.

Malcolm, then, sees Proslogion 3 as presenting different argument for God than Proslogion 2. While he agrees with Kant that existence is not a predicate that conveys anything meaningful about a concept, he does believe that necessary existence is a meaningful and important idea which can be used to prove the existence of God.

> A number of specialist terms have been used throughout this response.

AO2

Evaluating and utilising the associated Triggers for the specific controversy over the effectiveness of challenges to the ontological argument.

An introduction is not required for an AO2 response; this response is effective in that it 'dives right in' and responds directly to the area.

The monk Gaunilo, a contemporary of Anselm, attempted to strike at the core of Anselm's argument by showing it to be an absurd form of arguing. He did this by substituting 'the most excellent island' for God. According to Anselm's logic, if one believed that (i) existence in reality was greater than something existing only in the mind and (ii) that one could have the idea of a perfect island, then this island would have to exist in reality. Yet, we know that this is absurd, therefore Anselm has created a word game which proves nothing.

However, there are two problems with Gaunilo's argument. The first is that 'the most excellent island' is not equivalent to Anselm's 'that-which-nothing-greater-can-be-conceived'. Gaunilo's argument would be more effective if he had stated 'an island than which nothing greater can be conceived'. Yet, even if he had done this, he would have missed the core of Anselm's argument in Proslogion 3: an island cannot be compared to God, because an island does not have necessary existence, only contingent existence. Anything with contingent existence lies outside of Anselm's argument. This seems to be a very strong rebuttal to Gaunilo because it means that contingent subjects cannot be substituted for God in a critique of Anselm's argument.

This paragraph ends with a 'mini-conclusion'; this demonstrates evaluative ability.

In the 18th century, Immanuel Kant shared a criticism of Descartes' formulation of the ontological argument which many have found effective. Descartes had asserted that God was a being who contained all perfections and that 'all perfections' included existence. Kant believed that if we considered the nature of predicates, this would reveal that Descartes' argument was composed of nothing more than empty words. Predicates are that part of a sentence which contain a verb as well as something about the subject. For example, if we consider the assertion 'The car in that parking lot is blue', the predicate 'is blue' tells us something quite definite about the car. For, if we were trying to find a car in a vast parking lot, 'blue' might be a critical part of the information we would need to locate that car. Kant questioned 'exists' as a predicate, for 'exists' adds nothing new to our understanding of the car. Kant said that if we consider 100 thalers (a currency in Kant's time), it makes no difference to our understanding of the concept if the thalers are real or imaginary – it is still 100 thalers. Some might try to defend Descartes by saying that a 'non-existing God' is indeed different than an 'existing God'; however, it seems that one cannot simply just declare 'existence' to be a perfection when we do not use the term 'existence' in this way with any other thing or concept that we describe.

Some of the Triggers used in this paragraph are from the AO1 section – candidates should use any Triggers that help them answer the question.

Here is a second 'mini-conclusion' – this shows that evaluation is fully present in this response.

Both challenges from Gaunilo and Kant appear to be effective because they work with concepts with which we are familiar. For, if we are going to accept an argument for God's existence, we must be able to understand that argument outside of its specific application.

However, Gaunilo's challenge fails on two counts: he does not express his ideas in an equivalent way and he does not meet the argument presented in Proslogion 3. Kant's challenge, as we have seen, is much more effective. It challenges the attempt to use 'existence' to describe anything – including God. If Kant's challenge is accepted, then the ontological argument must be dismissed as a word game. Believers may object, declaring that that God belongs in a **unique** category all by Him/Her/Itself and that therefore the ontological argument should be accepted. However, the only thing that Kant (and this essay) can agree with is that if there is a God, then he contains all perfections. As Kant said, '… the famous ontological argument of Descartes is therefore merely so much labour and effort lost …' This means that all of the argumentation employed has never succeeded in moving us beyond an 'if'.

> There is a clear conclusion that flows from points made earlier. Note the effective use of a part of a Trigger quote.

T3: **Some areas for examination**

An answer using the Triggers to assist in explaining the logical problem of evil.

AO1

One of the major problems with belief in a God is reconciling this belief with all the evil and suffering in the world. Traditional theism believes in a God who is **omnipotent** (therefore omniscient) and **benevolent**, which is not consistent with the **co-existence** of evil and suffering. Some would argue that the overwhelming scale and depth of evil and suffering, such as, for example, the millions of innocents killed in the Holocaust, is far too great to accept the claim that God exists.

> Each paragraph is focused on exactly what has been asked.

This problem, widely known as the problem of evil (though the problem of **suffering** might perhaps be a more apt name, as it extends to all sorts of suffering **experience**) has long been a major cause for questioning God's existence, but it was first stated as an argument by the Greek philosopher Epicurus. He argued: 'Either God wants to abolish evil, and cannot; or he can, but does not want to. If he wants to, but cannot, he is impotent. If he can, but does not want to, he is wicked.'

> A Trigger quote has been used to strengthen this response.

The conclusion is that given the indisputable evidence of great, and often clearly needless, suffering in the world, God cannot logically have all three attributes, or he may not exist at all. In practice, even if God's omniscience is limited by the objection that he cannot know all the evil the future has in store, there are some continuing current evils in the world, like flooding and starvation, in which any truly benevolent God would be expected to intervene.

Since omnipotence, omniscience and benevolence are three absolutely fundamental properties of the God of classical theism (that is the God of three major monotheistic world religions, Christianity, Judaism and Islam), the problem of evil poses a major philosophical question that any religious believer must answer.

An additional factor which strengthens the problem of evil is that God is supposed to have created the world. Yet it is an uncaring world, with not only a number of species in fierce, ruthless and often bloody competition with each other, but also instances of **natural 'evil'** such as volcanoes and earthquakes. It could well be asked why God chose to create these features, surely unavoidable to an omnipotent creator, as they create great, completely indiscriminate suffering for which no human can be blamed, and against which humans have been utterly helpless for much of history.

> No judgement has been made as to the validity of the argument as this would not be appropriate for an 'explain' question/AO1 response.

AO2

Evaluating, and utilising the associated Triggers for the specific controversy over the effectiveness of an Augustinian type theodicy.

> Note use of AO1 triggers to set the context. This is a valid approach.

Augustine claimed that God made a perfect world, but that humans turned away from God of their own **free will**, and that that is how evil and suffering came into the world. This obviously has a biblical basis in the story of Adam committing the **original sin** of eating the fruit of the tree of knowledge of good and evil, and as, according to Augustine, we were all **'seminally present'** in Adam, he argues that we are all bear the guilt of his sin. This is also why there is **natural evil** in the world, with earthquakes and volcanoes, as the created order was affected by this original sin. Augustine also claims that evil is not a real **substance** and that it is a **privation of good**, a falling short of perfection. Finally, the **felix culpa** or 'happy mistake' brings hope through Christ in that belief brings salvation.

> This answer does not use an introduction to state an overall position. It is perfectly valid to 'jump right in' to the issues of an AO2 question and come to a position at the end. It is also valid to begin a response by stating a position.

But there are a number of problems with this argument. First of all, it is hard to see how God's creation went so wrong if God created it perfect. As the philosopher Schleiermacher pointed out, the evil must have come from somewhere, but if God created the whole world, as perfect (as was clearly possible for an omnipotent being, and as Augustine claims) there could be no way for it to have gone wrong.

> This paragraph presents strengths and weaknesses of a particular point, ending with a mini-conclusion.

Secondly, and most importantly, Augustine's argument has simply been superseded by science. Volcanoes have been on the surface of the earth for aeons before humans ever emerged and are governed by natural laws that that operate regardless of human suffering. The blind, uncaring nature of these natural laws and of nature generally make this look very unlike the sort of world God would create.

There is also the issue with Adam and Eve as the first original human beings making the literal idea of original sin questionable. It is today recognised as a very unusual and unsubstantiated moral notion that children should be punished for the sins of their parents. The idea of being 'seminally present' in Adam and being equally responsible for his sin is widely rejected by modern science.

> This paragraph makes use of Trigger words from the AO1 section in order to explain the point. This is followed by a criticism of this same point.

There is no doubt that the evidence against God as classical theism dictates is very strong. The logical problem of evil does pose a major problem at face value. But some, like Augustine, may argue that the problem is only apparent when a superficial overview is taken. Augustine's theodicy has certainly proven popular with believers and his explanation does meet the problems initially set. However, there are more problems than just the straightforward logical equations and the issue of whether or not God created evil. Another challenge to the effects of the Fall on the created order is the issue of animal suffering. Whilst Augustine can readily explain animal suffering in terms of human moral evil and natural evil (disease etc.) the theodicy does not reflect attitudes today towards animals. Why did other beings suffer because of a human mistake? It appears they are innocent victims. Why are not animals offered the same opportunity of redemption as humans are? In light of heightened sensitivity towards animals today Augustinian type theodicies may not satisfy a modern audience.

> The Trigger quote in this paragraph is made effective by an explanation of its meaning.

It is for this reason that I feel that whilst at one level Augustine can justify the traditional idea of God in the light of evil, it is not this that becomes the major obstacle. Indeed, until religious believers can answer these more direct questions above, the traditional idea of God as being all-loving, just and all-powerful will always have a dark cloud of uncertainty lingering above it.

> This paragraph reaches a detailed and reasoned conclusion which effectively uses points made earlier in the response.

T4: Some areas for examination

An answer using the Triggers to assist in explaining conversion experiences in relation to other religious experiences.

AO1

Conversion is the type of religious experience in which a subject has a 'turning around' in their beliefs or orientation to the divine. There is a relationship between conversion and other religious experiences, as a conversion may be the result of prayers, or happen after a mystical experience or vision. An example of this interrelationship is the conversion of the Apostle Paul which followed a vision of Jesus; the brief dialogue between Jesus and Paul in this vision might even be described as a prayer (Acts 9).

> This response directly addresses the question.

Conversions can be individual or communal. The example (above) of Paul is an individual conversion experience. A more contemporary example is the conversion of the scholar and popular writer, C. S. Lewis

> This response explores one example in depth, using a Trigger quote and a number of specialist terms.

> A wide variety of examples are used throughout this answer. This paragraph makes a relevant synoptic link.

> Key points are always supported by evidence or examples.

> There is no need for a conclusion; every paragraph has responded directly to the question.

who traces his sudden change to a specific time: 'In the Trinity Term of 1929 I gave in, and admitted that God was God, and knelt and prayed.' Note the words 'gave in' – this conveys a sense of dramatic change which is an aspect of conversion experiences. Lewis' experience could be called '**self-surrendering**' as it occurred after a period of resistance in contrast to a more willing (or **volitional**) conversion experience. Note also that prayer is an aspect of the experience, thus showing that different religious experiences can occur at the same time.

However, not all conversions are solitary. There are times when a group of people will respond in a dramatic way to a message. This is the case in the book of Acts with the crowd 'repenting' (from metanoia, the Greek word for change) after listening to Peter's sermon. A more recent example are the transformations of many church communities in Wales during the **Welsh revivals** of 1904–05. These and many other cases of conversion (though not all) involve an experience of the 'Word of God' as an inspired source, with subjects sensing God speaking directly through the Bible – this links to the 'objective view' of inspiration believed in by many Christians.

Conversion experiences can be **sudden or gradual**. Indeed, they might be described as both at the same time. For, the moment of a sudden conversion could have been preceded by weeks, months or years of searching, longing, questions, and encounters which all could have been, subconsciously moving the subject to a moment of change. This is certainly the case with Augustine who had been contemplating the truth of Christianity years prior to his conversion experience.

Conversion experiences are not always from atheism to faith as it was for C. S. Lewis. They involve other **types** such as moving from one faith to another (Muhammed Ali), from faith-believing to faith-trusting (John Wesley), and from an immoral, wayward life to finding the strength to live in the way one wishes (Augustine).

AO2

Evaluating, and utilising the associated Triggers for the specific controversy over the adequacy of William James' categories of mystical experience.

William James' categories of mystical experience are of tremendous value because they come from an **objective** point of view. James' goal was to cast a broad net over a variety of experiences and identify common elements rather than merely accept how these experiences are described by any one religion. The fact that his categories have been admired and used by numerous scholars (such as F. C. Happold and N. Smart) and continue to be discussed today (more than a century later) is evidence that they have succeeded in providing a framework for these experiences. It could be argued, however, that James' work is not as objective as it appears. For, he did not engage in quantitative research, but selected most of his examples from **literary sources** with no apparent justification. Many of his examples are from the **Christian tradition** and they are individual rather than communal in nature. Is James shaping the very phenomenon he seeks to describe? Based on the arbitrary and limited nature of the data used, it is difficult to think of James being an objective researcher.

> This paragraph presents strengths and weaknesses of a particular point, ending with a mini-conclusion.

Yet James' four categories succeed in applying neutral terms to the experiences conveyed by those who are universally described as 'mystics'. For example, these mystics express a sense of **passivity** in the face of divine power and a definite beginning and ending to a powerful, but short experience (**transiency**). Furthermore, those who have studied the writings of the mystics will surely agree with James that these subjects express what they feel to be important messages (**noetic quality**) but at the same time share a sense that they have had an encounter that defies full expression (**ineffability**). Yet, is it not strange that James did not include the sense of 'oneness' as a unifying testimony between all mystics? For mystics across religions (from Meister Eckart to Sufi mysticism, Al-Hallaj and Guru Nanak) speak of their experience of oneness with the divine, leading F. C. **Happold** to add 'unity of opposites' to James' list (along with timelessness and a sense of finding one's true self).

> This paragraph makes use of Trigger words from the AO1 section in order to explain the point. This is followed by a criticism of this same point.

Perhaps the biggest challenge to James' categories comes from those who do not consider it possible to apply universal categories to experiences – whether or not they are religious. For, every experience takes place in a **cultural context** – historical, linguistic, geographical, technological, etc. The **assumption** that we can simply ignore those factors and apply a label to an experience does not do justice to the particularity of experiences and gives us a false sense that we are understanding a report when it would actually require an immersion into the context of the subject of the mystical experience. Stephen Katz articulates this objection when he says, '...the experience itself ... is shaped by concepts which the mystic brings to, and which shape, his experience'. Katz is referring to the fact that there is simply no such thing as an uninterpreted experience. The moment we begin to use words, we are already interpreting. James, then, gives us a false sense of objectivity when, really, each mystical experience is unique and must be uniquely understood.

> The Trigger quote in this paragraph is made effective by an explanation of its meaning.

There are just too many difficulties, then, to see James' views as providing an adequate framework for mystical experience. In fact, when Happold adds three more categories to James' work, we might see this as the beginning of a 'slippery slope' in which one will have to end up adding as many categories as there are mystics in order to fully understand these experiences in their contexts. This is because there can never by a single valid interpretation of experiences which span both centuries and cultures.

> This paragraph reaches a reasoned conclusion which effectively uses points made earlier in the response.

Synoptic links

The table below contains suggestions for *some* synoptic links that can be made in relation to specific issues for Year 1 Philosophy of Religion. Remember (i) using synoptic links is not a 'tick-box' exercise; only use a link if it is directly relevant to the point you are trying to explain in an AO1 response or an argument you are making in an AO2 response. (ii) The table below is not exhaustive; candidates may find more links than are listed here.

Theme/subtheme/description	Possible synoptic links
1.A. Inductive arguments – cosmological: Inductive proofs; the concept of 'a posteriori'. Cosmological argument: St Thomas Aquinas' first Three Ways – (motion or change; cause and effect; contingency and necessity). The Kalam cosmological argument with reference to William Lane Craig (rejection of actual infinities and concept of personal creator).	• Aquinas crops up all over the Specification, especially in Ethics! • Challenges to religion from Science (YR2 all religions) • Kalam is an Islamic concept • The authority of religious texts (YR1 and YR2 all religions)
1.B. Inductive arguments – teleological: St Thomas Aquinas' Fifth Way - concept of governance; archer and arrow analogy. William Paley's watchmaker – analogy of complex design. F. R. Tennant's anthropic and aesthetic arguments – the universe specifically designed for intelligent human life.	• Challenges to religion from Science (YR2 all religions) • The authority of religious texts (YR1 and YR2 all religions)
1.C. Challenges to inductive arguments: David Hume – empirical objections and critique of causes (cosmological). David Hume – problems with analogies; rejection of traditional theistic claims: designer not necessarily God of classical theism; apprentice god; plurality of gods; absent god (teleological). Alternative scientific explanations including Big Bang theory and Charles Darwin's theory of evolution by natural selection.	• Challenges to religion from Science (YR2 all religions) • The authority of religious texts (YR1 and YR2 all religions)
2.A. Deductive arguments – origins of the ontological argument Deductive proofs; the concept of 'a priori'. St Anselm – God as the greatest possible being (Proslogion 2). St Anselm – God has necessary existence (Proslogion 3).	• The definition of God given in the ontological argument can be compared or contrasted with the definition of God/the Divine/Ultimate Reality in the religion under study (Buddhism. Christianity, Hinduism, Islam, Judaism or Sikhism)
2.B. Deductive arguments – developments of the ontological argument: Rene Descartes – concept of God as supremely perfect being; analogies of triangles and mountains/valleys. Norman Malcolm – God as unlimited being: God's existence as necessary rather than just possible.	• The nature of God (Christianity YR1) • The concept of Allah (Islam YR1) • Beliefs about the nature of God/concept of God (Judaism YR1) • The nature of ultimate reality (Buddhism YR1) • Brahman and atman (Hinduism YR1) • Philosophical understanding of the Sikh concept of God (Sikhism YR1)
2.C. Challenges to the ontological argument: Gaunilo, his reply to St Anselm; his rejection of the idea of a greatest possible being that can be thought of as having separate existence outside of our minds; his analogy of the idea of the greatest island as a ridicule of St Anselm's logic. Immanuel Kant's objection – existence is not a determining predicate: it cannot be a property that an object can either possess or lack.	• The impassability of God (Christianity YR1) • The definition of God in the Qur'an 51:47 (Islam YR1) • God as eternal (Judaism YR1) • Pratityasamutpada vs. necessary existence (Buddhism YR1) • Brahman as being (Hinduism YR1) • God as nirguna (Sikhism YR1)
3.A. The problem of evil and suffering: The types of evil: moral (caused by free will agents) and natural (caused by nature). The logical problem of evil: classical (Epicurus) - the problem of suffering. J. L. Mackie's modern development - the nature of the problem of evil (inconsistent triad). William Rowe (intense human and animal suffering) and Gregory S. Paul (premature deaths).	• Key moral principles (YR1 and YR2 all religions) • The nature of God (nirvana in Buddhism) (YR1 and YR2 all religions) • Dukkha in Buddhism (YR1)

Theme/subtheme/description	Possible synoptic links
3.B. Religious responses to the problem of evil (i): Augustinian type theodicy: Evil as a consequence of sin: evil as a privation; the fall of human beings and creation; the Cross overcomes evil, soul-deciding; challenges to Augustinian type theodicies: validity of accounts in Genesis, Chapters 2 and 3; scientific error – biological impossibility of human descent from a single pair (therefore invalidating the 'inheritance of Adam's sin'); moral contradictions of omnibenevolent God and existence of Hell; contradiction of perfect order becoming chaotic – geological and biological evidence suggests the contrary.	• Key moral principles (YR1 and YR2 all religions) • The nature of God (nirvana in Buddhism) (YR1 and YR2 all religions) • Dukkha in Buddhism (YR1)
3.C. Religious responses to the problem of evil (ii): Irenaean type theodicy: Vale of soul-making: human beings created imperfect; epistemic distance; second-order goods; eschatological justification; challenges to Irenaean type theodicies: concept of universal salvation unjust; evil and suffering should not be used as a tool by an omnibenevolent God; immensity of suffering and unequal distribution of evil and suffering.	• Key moral principles (YR1 and YR2 all religions) • The nature of God (nirvana in Buddhism) (YR1 and YR2 all religions) • Dukkha in Buddhism (YR1)
4.A. The nature of religious experience with particular reference to: Visions – sensory; intellectual; dreams. Conversion – individual/communal; sudden/gradual. Mysticism – transcendent; ecstatic and unitive. Prayer – types and stages of prayer according to Teresa of Avila.	• The early church (conversion and prayer) (Christianity YR1) • Luther's conversion (Christianity YR1) • The community of believers – prayer (Christianity YR1) • The night of power as a vision (Islam YR1) • Shahada and conversion/reversion in Islam (Islam YR1) • Salah and other forms of prayer (Islam YR2) • Prayer in Judaism and synagogue as a place of prayer (Judaism YR2/YR1) • Enlightenment of the Buddha as a vision (Buddhism YR1) • Meditation and mindfulness in Buddhism (Buddhism YR1/YR2) • Practices of ISKON (Hinduism YR1) • Puja and Bhakti (Hinduism YR1/YR2) • Guru Nanak's experience of God's court (Sikhism YR1) • Role of the GGS (Sikhism YR1) • Naam Japo (Sikhism YR1)
4.B. Mystical experience: William James' four characteristics of mystical experience: ineffable, noetic, transient and passive. Rudolf Otto – the concept of the numinous; mysterium tremendum; the human predisposition for religious experience.	• The Charismatic movement (Christianity YR2) • Sufi thought and practices (Islam YR2) • Hasidism, esotericism, meditation and God's essence (Judaism YR2) • Awakening as beyond language (Buddhism YR1) • Zen koans (Buddhism YR1) • Advaita Vedanta; Relationship between brahman and atman (Hinduism YR1/YR2) • Ramakrishna's mysticism (Hinduism YR2) • The nature of the soul and monism (Sikhism YR1)
4.C. Challenges to the objectivity and authenticity of religious experience: With reference to Caroline Franks Davis (description-related; subject-related and object-related challenges). Claims of religious experience rejected on grounds of misunderstanding; claims delusional – possibly related to substance misuse, fantastical claims contrary to everyday experiences. Challenges: individual experiences valid even if non-verifiable; claims could be genuine – integrity of individual; one-off experiences can still be valid even if never repeated.	• Challenges from science (Christianity YR2) • Challenges to Islam from science (Islam YR1) • Challenges to Judaism from science (Judaism YR1) • Buddhism as a secular philosophy (Buddhism YR1) • Challenges to Sikhism from science (Sikhism YR2)

AO1 responses: essential guidance

These insights will help you to meet the WJEC/Eduqas criteria for knowledge and understanding in an examination setting.

1. Make sure your first sentence responds directly to the question.

You will then maintain this same focus throughout your answer. For example, if you are responding to a question which asks you to explain the religious experience of visions in relation to other experiences, your first sentence might be, 'A vision involves seeing something beyond normal experience; this could happen in prayer, a mystical experience or even in as a part of a conversion experience.'

2. You do not need an introduction or conclusion for an AO1 question.

Having an introduction or conclusion may mean that you end up repeating information or including material that is not relevant – this material will not gain you any extra marks. For example, if you are asked to explain Otto's concept of the numinous, you might be tempted to begin with an explanation of religious experience in general along with some biblical examples. However, doing this is not a response to the question. Rather, you should begin by directly discussing Otto's key ideas and contributions. Only after this will you set this in a larger context.

3. Know how to use quotations correctly.

A relevant quote can strengthen an explanation in an AO1 response – that's why 'Trigger quotes' have been included in this guide. But do not let the quote do the work for you. Always include an explanation of the quotation and why it is important for the explanation you are making. For instance, in a response that examines the challenges to religious experience (4.C.) you could include a Trigger quote from Franks Davis (just under the AO1 Triggers for that section). Make sure that you include a sentence remarking on the meaning of the quote or how it relates to the question that has been asked. Remember: quotes are not necessary; you can, instead, paraphrase key ideas.

4. **Use scholars, examples and sources as often as possible to explain key points.**

Of course, there are themes where there are no scholars mentioned in the Specification (such as 4.A.); here, you will want to ensure you are very familiar with sacred texts, sources of authority (Teresa of Avila), and examples used in the textbook. However, in other sections (such as 4.B.) where both James and Otto are named in relation to mysticism) you will want to ensure you can speak about each scholar in depth; if they have used examples, illustrations or key ideas (such as James' 4 characteristics or Otto's *mysterium tremendum*) you can explore these in order to show that you grasp their viewpoints in depth.

5. **Include specialist language in your answer.**

This is a sign that you have studied an area with depth. However, you will not be awarded any marks for 'dropping terms' into an answer when it is clear that you do not know the meaning of the words you are using. For instance, if you were using the phrase '*mysterium trememdum et fascinans*' to describe Otto's views you would want to make sure you indicated you knew this term by discussing how Otto sees two different emotional reactions to a numinous experience – fear/awe as well as fascination.

6. **Wandering into biographical details or related subjects – when this is not asked for by the question – will hold you back.**

If, for example, you are asked to explain the meaning of mystical experiences alone and include a discussion of the birthplace and family relationships of William James, this will not gain you any marks – even if the information you have shared is accurate. Always remain focused on the question.

7. **For Year 2 students: include a synoptic link, but only where appropriate.**

This means including an idea from one of the other two areas of the course. For instance, if you are asked to examine challenges to religious experience, you may want to bring in some of the challenges from science to the religion you have studied when these criticisms apply to claims for religious experience. How many links do you need in a paper? There is no magic number. Indeed, trying to force a link that doesn't quite 'fit' or use a formula will weaken your paper; you would be better off not attempting a synoptic link. However, a single, well-placed link in an answer will be fulfilling the highest band: 'insightful connections are made between the various approaches studied'.

These insights will help you to meet the WJEC/Eduqas criteria for evaluation in an examination setting.

1. Delve into evaluative issues, engaging with the material you present.
The heart of your paper is your examination of controversies relevant to the question with attention to scholars and/or sources of wisdom. This is why three controversies have been outlined for you with every issue. For example, if you need to make an evaluative response to the issue of the extent to which the Kalam cosmological argument is convincing, you can be guided by the three controversies that are outlined for this area in the Evaluation sections of 1.A.

2. Support your evaluation with quotes, references and examples.
For example, your presentation of a controversy will be strengthened by including a relevant Trigger quote from this text. Let's say you are presenting the controversy over the whether or not inductive arguments for God's existence are persuasive. This is the first controversy from the 'Evaluation section for this issue in 1.A. You can support your evaluation by using one of the Trigger quotes underneath the controversies from Mackie or Dawkins. Your job would be to show how the quote speaks to this controversy.

3. Continually review and reflect on the arguments you present.
In other words, don't hold all of your conclusions until the end of the paper. For example, you can add a mini-conclusion to the discussion of a specific controversy. Come to a provisional viewpoint on just one of the controversies you are covering prior to your overall conclusion at the end of the answer. Let's say that you are examining the effectiveness of the teleological argument for God's existence. You can wrap up that part of the discussion up with a mini conclusion: 'Maybe the rejection of God as an explanation equally requires a measure of faith in highly improbable scientific evidence? It all depends on whether one accepts or rejects the proposal by some physicists and mathematicians that in an infinite universe, whatever is possible will eventually occur.' This is a provisional conclusion; you might even disagree with it in your final conclusion, but it shows that your 'evaluative brain' is engaged throughout your answer.

4. **A short introduction can set a great tone.**
It is not necessary to have an introduction, but a few sentences at the beginning of the paper that include specialist language and an indication of some of the relevant issues you are going to examine can help the examiner see that you are 'in the zone'. Stating a position in the introduction is optional. Some students declare a position on an issue at the beginning of their response and then 'check in' on that position as they move through their response. It is equally acceptable to not come to a position until the end of the answer.

5. **Be fair to positions that are not your own.**
One sign of strong evaluative ability is to represent positions that are not your own fairly and with depth. One way to practise doing this is to adopt a position that is not your own. For example, if you consider that teleological arguments are not relevant to the 21st century, ensure that you have included some strong arguments believers might have for considering the relevance of the teleological argument today (i.e. the anthropic and aesthetic principles proposed by Tennant).

6. **Conclude by stating a position and justifying it.**
This position may be stated in the 'third person' ('It seems clear that ...') or in the first person ('I think that ...' or 'I believe that ...') However, what is most important is that this statement is followed by a justification for your position. You can do this by looking back at the various arguments you have presented and also at your 'mini conclusions'. Then, restate these in a new way.

7. **For Year 2 students: include a synoptic link, but only where appropriate.**
This means bringing an idea in from one of the other two areas of the course. For instance, if you are writing an answer to the issue of the effectiveness of the challenges to the cosmological/teleological argument for God's existence (Theme 1.C.), you might find it natural to bring in the ideas found in the nature of God sections of the world religions. How many links are needed in a response? There is no magic number. Indeed, trying to 'shoe-horn' a link that doesn't really 'fit in' will weaken your paper; you would be better off without trying this. However, one well-placed link in an answer will fulfil one of the requirements of the highest band: 'insightful connections are made between the various approaches studied'.

Index

Index